# Learning to Hear God's Voice

## My Journey

### by
### Rebecca L. Hein

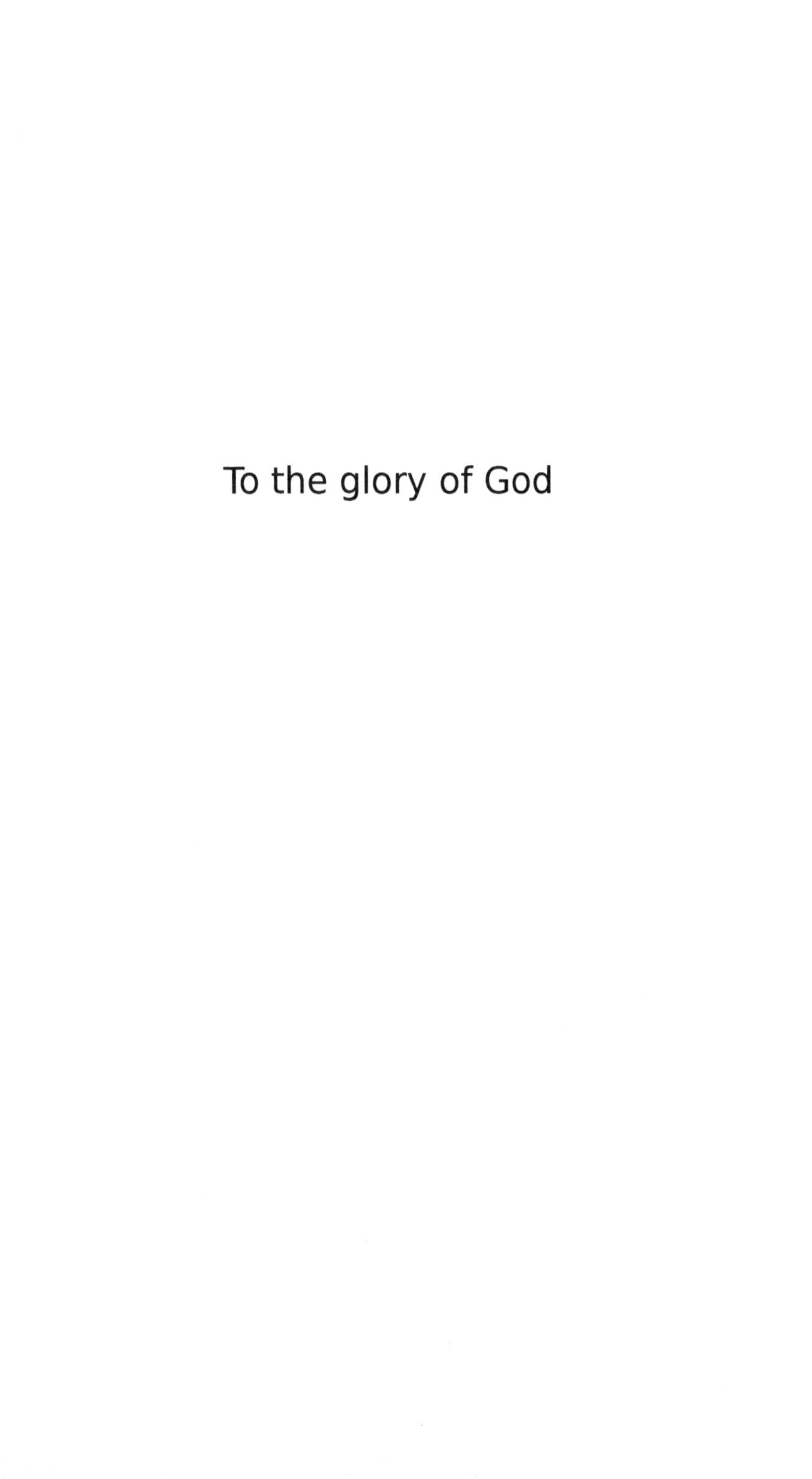

To the glory of God

"God's law is not a thing, an 'it,' but it is a relationship involving a divine speaker who must be heard and answered."
Lewis Benson

# Table of contents


1--Beginning as an atheist     1

2--Struggling with false religion     9

3--Reading the Journal of George Fox     17

4--Reading Catholic Quakerism     21

5--Help at a difficult juncture  27

6--Confronting fear     31

7--My battle with fear: God's purpose     39

8--Learning complete obedience     45

9--Learning complete trust     51

10--Freedom from sin     57

11--More about freedom from sin     65

12--Help with my anniversary reactions     73

13--Whose approval?     83

14--Finding the wisdom of God     91

15--The pearl of great value   99

16--The supremacy of God's help     105

17--A lesson about discernment      109

18--Receiving a miracle          113

19--Who knows the most?        119

20--"It is not a sin to be tempted."   127

21--Deliverance   131

# Chapter 1
# Beginning as an atheist

"Behold, I stand at the door and knock." Rev. 3:20 (All Scripture references are from the Revised Standard Version of the Bible.)

Fear gripped my entrails as I clutched the phone receiver, trying to take in the bad news about my sister.

"Cathy was rushed to the emergency room last night in terrible pain. When they operated, they found a grapefruit-sized tumor in each ovary—and on one side it was starting to grow out."

First our grandmother, then our mother, now Cathy. Would I be next?

But there was more. Among the different types of ovarian cancer, it turned out that Mom's and Cathy's were the same. Our grandmother's records were lost.

Facing this conclusive evidence that a

hereditary disease stalked our family, I shot into panic. I could only hope that God would see me through what was coming.

Seven years ago, in 1981, I'd been an atheist. My first experience of church occurred in mid-to-late grade school, when Cathy attended a Presbyterian church for a few months, and brought me along. Our atheist parents belonged to the local Unitarian Fellowship, in Casper, Wyoming.

The confusion and boredom of church resumed when I began playing the cello in various church services, in late high school and college. Nothing in Christianity or in any other religion attracted me.

I'd concluded that Christians were sanctimonious hypocrites who pushed their point of view, and this attitude was bolstered by my occasional encounters with members of Jews for Jesus or Campus Crusade for Christ.

But by 1981, I'd begun thinking about my world without a God in it. For weeks I turned this over in my mind, and finally saw a mental picture of my condition: My consciousness was swimming around in my head like a goldfish in a bowl, but the bowl had no opening. It was clear glass. I could see out upon the world but was stuck inside.

With no entrance or exit, this was profound, existential loneliness that other people's company could not alleviate. Therefore I saw that if God existed, I needed him.

Next I began wondering how I could prove or disprove his existence. I was then twenty-five, and attending graduate school at Northwestern University in Evanston, Illinois.

I lived about six blocks west of campus, and every day that fall, pacing back and forth to my classes and rehearsals in the music building on the edge of Lake Michigan, I pondered the question. I'd walk under huge old maples and oaks, brilliant with red and yellow leaves, thinking, *How can I know for sure if God exists?*

Weeks passed, and I began to feel stuck. Then one day, walking to class as usual, I saw my choice: In my mind's eye, two identical vases were sitting on either end of a large mantel. One represented proof of God's existence, the other, proof of his non-existence. I could never prove either one.

In that moment I decided to believe in God, walking across a line so clear to me that it might as well have been drawn across the sidewalk. Years later I recalled this episode, and realized that God, in knocking at the door of my soul, had spoken to me through the pictures of the closed fishbowl and the vases on the mantel.

Around this time, I dreamed I was sitting on a couch with a close friend. This loving being knew me better than I knew myself, and our communion was instantaneous and perfect. I had a spark of this being within myself that shone with recognition as he spoke to me.

We were recalling something wrong I'd recently done; nothing major, perhaps a white lie. In our moment of mutual recollection, I knew he had forgiven me, and that any worse sin would have been equally forgiven.

I also felt a clear sense that the small magnitude of my sin was just as serious as a major act of wrongdoing would have been. All this, my intimate friend conveyed to me with tenderness and laughter. I woke up thinking, *If there is such a Being, I want to know Him better.*

I felt that this dream had confirmed the existence of God and that he loved me. My next burning questions were: What is the importance of Jesus Christ? Is he really the only way to God?

I knew I needed God; I hated men—all men. Because of a few bad experiences, including having had an alcoholic father and an abusive boyfriend, I'd begun to blame men for all my problems, helped down this dark path by radical feminist writings I'd read while researching a paper in undergraduate school.

Yet I knew it was unjust to blame a whole group of people for the evils of a few. So my sense of fairness fought with my deeper feelings, exhausting my emotions and locking me into a battle I could never win.

My hatred was more powerful than I: This conviction grew alongside my desire to know for certain whether Jesus is the only way to

God. I began to sense that God would again require me to decide ahead of any sort of proof.

However, this time my indecision was prolonged because I felt that any single way to God left many people out, and that seemed unfair and not characteristic of a loving God. So my struggle of belief dragged on for months while I continued in hate, wanting out but not seeing the way.

I was reading the Bible at the time. In Gen. 19:58, I found the story of Sodom and Gamorrah, in which Lot is cast as a "righteous man." Men come to Lot's house asking for men they can have sex with. Instead, Lot offers his two virgin daughters, saying, "[D]o to them as you please."

Lot was exposing his daughters to rape. I concluded that God approved; why else would he designate Lot a righteous man? Despite having recently read so many radical feminist writings, I was decades away from understanding the cultural and historical context of the Bible, in which the status of women was probably lower than cattle. Of course I couldn't tolerate this passage.

Worse yet was Matt. 5:39: "[I]f any one strikes you on the right cheek, turn to him the other also."

Apparently, God sanctioned my sick relationship with my college boyfriend. I could see no other interpretation.

Facing this irreconcilable conflict between

the close friend I'd met in my dream and the apparent attitudes of God I was finding in the Bible, I dropped my idea that "The Bible is my source of information about God."

For months I pondered the importance of Jesus Christ, and prayed about how he could be the only way for everyone. Then I saw that we all have unique personal histories, and therefore distinct paths. God can meet each of us on our own journey, which isn't anyone else's.

So Jesus could be the only way to God for everyone because there could be as many ways to God through Jesus as there are people in the world. If he is the universal way—the way for all people—that's the opposite of leaving people out. There doesn't need to be more than one way, if that way is for everyone.

Having seen this, I realized one evening that I could believe that Jesus is the only way to the Father. I'd just gone to bed and closed my eyes when a vision of power opened up before me.

I saw a whirling ball of dried-up mud, and knew it was my hatred. I was standing next to it with an ice pick in my hand, chipping away at it, when a voice said, "It must be attacked from the inside."

It exploded, and I found myself in outer space with fragments of that ball hurtling past me. A sound of retching and choking filled my ears, and I knew I was in deadly danger if one of those fragments hit me. A tiny piece had the same power to destroy me as a large one did. Next, I heard the gospel song "He's Got the Whole World in His Hands," and felt myself lifted out of that storm of hate.

Sure enough, as the days and weeks followed, I could feel that my spirit was liberated from the resentment and grudge-holding against all men, innocent or guilty, with which I'd struggled for so long. It was wonderful to be free, and I knew that if I wanted this to continue, I must pursue my relationship with Jesus.

# Chapter 2
# Struggling with false religion

I began by attending the Evanston Meeting of the Religious Society of Friends, whose long silences gave me the space I needed to hear from God. Eventually I became a member.

After about a year of attending this meeting, knowing I'd been in direct, regular contact with God, I'd become convinced that Jesus was the only guide and teacher I needed. Near the end of that year, I moved away to take a job in Oshkosh, Wisconsin.

This community had a tiny Quaker meeting, and I soon discovered that these few people were embroiled in a longstanding power struggle; it paralyzed the meeting and repelled newcomers, me included. Besides, I wanted Christian fellowship, something neither meeting had provided.

This search began shortly after I moved and was still attending Oshkosh Meeting. I made two mistakes: 1) I decided that anyone who professed to be a Christian probably was, and therefore I could learn from him or her 2) I assumed I could learn the most from those who appeared to be the most serious about their faith.

It didn't occur to me that I should be "as wise as a serpent and as innocent as a dove." (Matt. 10:16) Rather, I uncritically accepted what others told me about God, and attended several different churches in an attempt to open my heart to what the pastor was saying and to the whole church service and whatever else God had to say to me through it.

Yet instead of gaining a sense that I was hearing from God, I felt more and more that I was play-acting. When the congregation prayed together, that is, all spoke the same words at the same time, addressed to God, I knew that those words did not come from my heart. Singing hymns was even worse; I felt like a liar because I was mouthing words that did not express my condition.

I also began to hear an inner voice prompting me toward good behavior. For example, when my colleagues in the University of Wisconsin Oshkosh music department where I taught cello wasted rehearsal time gossiping, I tried not to participate.

I also heard that voice saying, "count others better than yourself." (Phil. 2:3) There were additional instances and, since this voice always counseled right action and also quoted Scripture, I figured it was the voice of God.

For months I worked hard to regulate my behavior and attitude, with increasing dreariness. This culminated at the end of a few weeks' Bible study on the book of James which Samantha, one of my new friends, had suggested.

I'd been feeling desperate and miserable about my mother's health. Nearly a year previously, she'd been diagnosed with late-stage ovarian cancer, and her prognosis was bad.

Nonetheless, chemotherapy had appeared to be working until approximately eight months after her initial surgery and diagnosis. Then she began feeling worse, and tests confirmed that the cancer was growing again.

Many people had been praying for my mother, who was only fifty-four when diagnosed, and it appeared to me that God was doing nothing. In the Bible study, we read, "Count it all joy...when you meet various trials." (James 1:2) This became one of the most mocking, burdensome inner admonitions I carried with me all day long.

Worse yet, when I told Samantha, who already knew my mother was not a Christian, that she was succumbing to the cancer, and expressed my bewilderment that God was doing nothing, Samantha thought a moment, and replied, "Sometimes the Shepherd breaks the leg of a sheep to keep it from straying."

The next person I talked to was the liberal Lutheran Campus Ministry pastor, whose young son had spina bifida. We talked about suffering in the world, about disease, and why God wasn't answering the many prayers for my mother's healing. "He can't heal," this pastor said, "my son wouldn't be in a wheelchair if He could."

I fled those two conversations in the deepest distress and confusion I'd ever known. Was God a demon or just a weakling? Neither fit the reality of a loving, all-powerful Creator who holds the whole universe in his hands.

Returning to my apartment, I lay down on my couch, crying for my mother and praying for help. I saw that my life had dwindled to a slow, gray trudge, and that I was dogged with Scriptural commands I could never obey.

Where was God? Where was the Being who had told me he loved me and who had delivered me from the bondage of hate? I felt that he had deserted me and could know nothing of my woes because he had never been a human being.

Then I remembered Jesus' words on the cross: "My God, my God, why hast thou forsaken me?" (Matt. 27:46) In a clear mental picture, I saw myself standing in darkness, staring at a thick veil. On the other side was brilliant light.

None of it could penetrate except by a pinhole that was my only way through. That pinhole was all I had in common with God:

Jesus' moment of despair. He was now, in truth, my only way to God.

Although this should have comforted me, I still felt heavy and disillusioned. Where had my earnest search taken me? Into false behavior, lies about God, and absolute discouragement. I realized that if these were the consequences of following God, it would be better not to believe in him at all.

So I became an atheist again. It was an instant change, taking complete hold of me the day after I saw the dark veil shutting me off from God's brilliant light. Since I was no longer bound by the strictures of that legal-istic inner voice, I gave myself license for any behavior I cared to indulge in.

But as the days passed, I noticed I didn't want to get drunk, nor to lie, cheat, or steal, nor to break any of God's other commandments. Instead, I felt happy and free, and this increas-ed to continuous jubilation.

However, the most important circumstance in my outward life had not changed: My mother was still sick, and as unlikely to improve as before. I was still sad about it, but that heavy cloud of doubt, duty, and constant striving had lifted.

I felt gratitude rising in me like the scent of flowers after a spring rain. This unbounded joy, I realized, should be the real fruit of following God, and within a few days I also saw that if the Lord was the author of this condition, he was someone I still wanted to know.

I continued throughout that school year, and into the summer of 1984, with a clear sense that my Creator and guide would not again allow me to mire myself in legalism and dim, choking duty. As to my search for fellowship, all I knew was that traditional churches had failed to fill that need, and even my sporadic attendance at liberal Quaker meetings would be another dead end.

The only hope of fellowship I'd found among Quakers was in the New Foundation Fellowship (NFF). Lewis Benson, then about seventy-five, had visited Evanston Friends Meeting during my last year there, along with a much younger man. He and his companion, both Quakers, re-proclaimed to us the Christian message of the early Friends, and spoke about the ministry of George Fox.

That was when I learned about the NFF, a loose group of Quakers dedicated to spreading Fox's message. But those people were widely scattered, and met only a few times per year. Benson's presentation intrigued me, and I began to think I should read the *Journal of George Fox*.

In mid-August of 1984, I found myself in my mother's hospital room in Casper. Mom was asleep or sedated. Earlier that day, her kidneys had failed, and she'd refused dialysis. We knew she could only live another few weeks.

As with other cancer patients, Mom had faced ups and downs, procedures and surgeries, and chemotherapy with its miserable side effects. It all added up to a nearly two-year mixture of hope, uncertainty and, for her, a slow downhill slide. Now she was dying.

I sat in the big upholstered recliner next to her bed and cried. Yet along with my grief, there was something else: God was there, pouring his love into me with a power beyond anything I'd ever known.

His presence was all around me, filling the room, filling my heart, calming and comforting me at this saddest of all moments, assuring me that all was well, even though I would soon have to part with my mother. I'd never felt such overpowering peace, and it went on and on. He did not need words to tell me that he was there, and that he loved me and my mom.

# Chapter 3
# Reading the Journal of
# George Fox

In the school year 1984-1985, I read the *Journal of George Fox*, edited by John L. Nickalls. Fox, commonly known as the founder of Quakerism, was born in 1624 in England. At nineteen, he left his family to to be alone and pray, seeking God. Early in this process, he found nothing in organized religion to guide or help him.

He wrote, "[P]rofessors [those who professed faith] took notice of me and sought to be acquainted with me, but I was afraid of them for I was sensible they did not possess what they professed." (Fox 1952, 3-4) He reported that in his search for God he was under "great misery and trouble" (Fox 1952, 4) for some years.

His "relations were much troubled at me that I would not go with them to hear the priests. [Church of England pastors] And I told them, 'Did not the apostle [John] say to believers that they needed no man to teach them, but as the anointing [within] teacheth them?'"

His relatives, though knowing this was in the Bible (1 John 2:27), and believing it, were still troubled that Fox "could not" go to church with them. Thus, added Fox, "I saw that a true believer was another thing than they looked upon it to be." (Fox 1952, 7-8)

I too had noticed the difference between God's direct speaking and what happened in church—and the viewpoint and apparent experience of churchgoers.

Fox struggled for several years, encountering "miserable comforters" who "brought my troubles more upon me." Then he had a major breakthrough, just as I had. (Fox 1952, 6)

He reported, "[W]hen all my hopes in... [religious people] were gone, so that I had nothing outwardly to help me...then, I heard a voice which said, 'There is one, even Christ Jesus, that can speak to thy condition', and when I heard it my heart did leap for joy." (Fox 1952, 11)

Not only did Fox share my experience, he added to my insights about errors embedded in human-made religion, starting with the apparent inner state of religious people. "I saw that professors, priests, and people were whole and at ease in that condition which was my misery." (Fox 1952, 12) Sure enough, at church I appeared to be the only person with reservations, both about the procedures and the underlying assumptions.

Fox also provided new insights: "And I saw the state of those, both priests and people, who in reading the Scriptures, cry out much against Cain, Esau, and Judas, and other wicked men of former times, mentioned in the Holy Scriptures; but do not see the nature of Cain, of Esau, of Judas, and those others, in themselves....I saw also how people read the Scriptures without a right sense of them, and without duly applying them to their own states." (Fox 1952, 30-31)

In addition, he explained to me why I'd had trouble understanding the Bible and, as we have seen, had emerged puzzled and confused from these efforts. "For I saw in that Light and Spirit which was before Scripture was given forth...that all must come to that Spirit, if they would know God, or Christ, or the Scriptures aright." (Fox 1952, 33)

In 1648, when he was about twenty-four, Fox received his commission to preach the Truth to the world. What follows is a brief excerpt, with the full text in the Appendix: "Now I was sent to turn people from darkness to the light that they might receive Christ Jesus....And I was to direct people to the Spirit that gave forth the Scriptures, by which they might be led into all Truth....I was to bring people off from all their own ways to Christ, the new and living way, and from their churches, which men had made and gathered...and off the world's teachers made by men, to learn of Christ." (Fox 1952, 34-35)

I hungered for this. Years ago, my journey of faith had begun with direct encounters with God, and I wanted these to continue. So I began to search for a better way than I'd found in church.

# Chapter 4
# Reading Lewis Benson's
# Catholic Quakerism

In the year I read Fox's Journal, I also read Benson's *Catholic Quakerism*. This book helped me to better understand Fox's message, and solved some of the most significant dilemmas I'd encountered while attempting to interact with churchgoers.

As we have seen, I struggled with Scriptural admonitions I couldn't obey, and was finally driven to despair. But in Benson's chapter, The Quaker Understanding of Christian Ethics, he states, "[T]hat which the eternal voice commands is never beyond our power to obey." (Benson 1983, 25)

This was a new idea to me. Contrasting the ethic of idealism with the ethic of obligation, he notes, "The Christian idealist sees morality as the struggle to attain ultimate moral goals, and he finds a wide gulf between these ultimate goals and...available moral energies....This approach takes it for granted that there can be an unresolvable tension between what a Christian knows he ought to do and what, in fact, he is able to do." Benson continued, "The ethic of obligation, on the other hand, sees right action as a response to God's command." (Benson 1983, 23-24)

I began to hope I could do what God required without again becoming trapped in legalism. Next I read, "The gap between the vision of moral truth and the power to do it is the bugbear of Protestant ethics, but it is totally absent from the teaching of Fox, [William] Penn and [Isaac] Penington. [Contemporaries of Fox] This leaves no room for the plea, 'I know what God wants me to do but I haven't the power to do it.'" (Benson 1983, 25)

Was I really going to escape my previous difficulties? Yes, I learned, reading on to the most important passage yet, which spelled out what I had to do: "Penington says, 'as the soul in faith gives itself up to obey, so the power appears and works the obedience...the power never fails the faith.'" (Benson 1983, 25)

I had never read anything like this in all the years I'd been trying to make sense of Christianity. But there was more. Benson clarified an important question I'd never been able to get any churchgoer to discuss: "[T]his encounter with moral truth [the voice of Christ] is not a private experience. God does not speak with two voices. The word of moral truth that comes to one comes to all....The turning of God's people to one living authority who teaches the same moral truth to all is an experience that brings all into unity." (Benson 1983, 30)

The church's many denominational splits had bothered me ever since I'd become a Christian, and now here was a clear statement of what's possible.

Along with leading me to these exciting discoveries, *Catholic Quakerism* motivated me to learn more about the NFF. In the Preface to the Fourth Printing, after describing how opportunities for spreading Fox's message had grown, Benson noted, "There is a growing number of people who have caught the 'Catholic [universal] Quaker' vision and...have found fellowship in the task of reproclaiming the everlasting gospel that Fox preached." Benson continued with Fox's core message, "Christ has come to teach his people himself." (Benson 1983, VIII-IX)

I found this powerful in its simplicity, and felt that any group that actually operated by listening to Christ, rather than by performing for him with programmed church services, group "prayers," hymn singing, and other human initiated practices, was a group I could be part of.

I also began to realize that a silent meeting for worship in the Name of Jesus, where all were gathered to listen to him, was completely different from the Quaker meetings for worship

I'd so far participated in, where often people appeared to pursue their own agendas.

So I became more and more curious about Meeting for Worship in the Name of Jesus, and longed to participate in such a meeting. Apparently I was not alone.

"Three centuries ago," Benson wrote in 1983, the early Quaker message "evoked in their hearers a burning desire to gather in Jesus' name, to wait to feel his presence.... [T]his same message is being preached to-day,...[and] is causing those who receive it to know Jesus in a personal encounter as they meet together to feel his presence." (Benson 1983, XI)

As the end of the 1984-85 academic year approached, I began to feel I should find a Quaker conference to attend during the coming summer, but I had no idea how to decide among the many possibilities. All year I'd been corresponding with Chris, the young man who had accompanied Benson on his visit to Evanston Meeting.

He suggested I attend the week-long New York Yearly Meeting session in August to hear Benson give one of the keynote addresses, and also to attend the Meetings for Worship in the Name of Jesus that the dozen or so NFF members there would be holding each day. I knew I wanted to hear whatever Benson had to say.

A Monthly Meeting convenes weekly for worship and once a month for business, typically involving those who regularly attend. Quarterly Meetings are both business meetings and administrative entities, and include attenders from several meetings in the region. Yearly Meetings gather once a year, and include all the Monthly Meetings in a designated geographical area—which might be a state, but could also include a larger area.

Benson's speech, given on the first evening, was clear, and inspired me, although it angered many people there. Next day, I met for worship with members of the NFF.

Less than five minutes into this meeting, I knew I was in the presence of the One who had come to me in my mother's hospital room almost a year before, only this time my sense of his love and power was increased a thousand fold. As God poured out his presence upon me, without stint or measure, I saw that this was the only thing the churches and the Yearly Meeting needed, and the one thing they did not have.

Here was the power to overcome any human problem, the source of love and unity for all Christians, the guide, the teacher, and the maker of order for any group that would listen to his voice.

From that time forward, my purpose in life was to spread the good news of the early Quaker gospel. Although visitations of such massive love and power did not recur, I continued to hear from God.

Most of these messages were admonitions to come out of my self-will and surrender to him completely. As time went on, I discovered that when I strayed, he warned me in unmistakable terms that I was in danger of choosing death over life; that such a choice could not be undone; and that I still had time to turn away from darkness and to listen to him with all my heart.

# Chapter 5
# Help at a difficult juncture

Wrapped in God's power and love, I drove west to visit my widowed father for the third and last time that summer. Preceding that visit, I'd made a series of unpleasant discoveries: Four months after Mom died, I flew home to spend the 1984 Christmas holidays with Dad, finding with dismay that Mom had been my buffer ever since I was born. But now she was gone, and during that whole week, I felt assaulted by the full force of his aggressive personality.

But it got worse: When I next visited him, in June 1985, I spent the entire first night I was there vomiting. I recovered quickly, but on the two-day drive back to Wisconsin, I had diarrhea all the way. The latter happened again, after the following visit about a month later.

Right after New York Yearly Meeting, Dad and I met in the Black Hills of South Dakota, where our family had owned a cabin ever since

I was twelve. It was the last cabin trip of that season. The afternoon we arrived, we did the usual chores: sweeping the floor, making the beds, and cleaning mouse droppings off the kitchen table and counter.

At suppertime I stood outside at our old wooden picnic table, cooking hamburgers and fried potatoes on our Coleman camp stove. A few wispy clouds floated overhead, and rays of late-afternoon sun were slanting through bunches of long pine needles bristling on every tree. Openings in the bark—roughly-edged ovals still sweet with the vanilla scent of fresh pine pitch—glowed golden in the light.

Behind me I heard the back screen door creak on its hinges as it opened, then closed.

"Here." Dad put two ceramic dinner plates on the tablecloth.

I leaned over to inspect them from my place in front of the hot skillet. "Dad, there's a mouse dropping on that plate. We'll have to wash it."

"Bah! What's a little mouse pellet? It's all dried up." Seizing the plate, he blew the dropping off onto the tablecloth and reached for the pancake turner to scoop a burger out of the pan.

"Give me that." I grabbed both plates. "You've been handling these dirty plates, so please wash your hands, then supervise the food while I clean up these dishes." But Dad reached for the pancake turner again. "Don't!" I yelled.

He knew I wouldn't stand for mouse-contaminated dishes. Therefore, he could make me jump like a token in a game of Tiddlywinks. I hated it, but could not bear to waste good food.

This episode was typical of a stay at the cabin with my father. If it wasn't about clean plates, it was about something else. I always fumed.

But this time it was different. Although I was as infuriated as ever, my rage did not lock up my gut or chest as usual, tightening muscles and probably raising my blood pressure. Instead, it coursed through me in powerful waves, which I could withstand in silence.

So I didn't need to struggle for self-control; rather, I waited in the presence and power of God, and the wave eventually subsided. Then another would hit, until my feelings were spent.

The silent release of all this anger was therapeutic. Rage at my father for a current episode or one long ago could make me sick, and had almost certainly caused my recent intestinal problems. But now I knew those waves meant I was no longer suppressing all that negative energy, only to have it blow out of my bowels a few days after I got away.

I was certain I wouldn't be sick again after spending time with my father, and I wasn't. Thus, God helped me to stay in this toxic relationship for many more years until he decided it was time for me to escape.

# Chapter 6
# Confronting fear

After that life-changing Meeting for Worship in the Name of Jesus, I began to learn all I could about the message and experience of the early Friends, also declaring that good news at every opportunity. During these years, starting in about 1986—the year after I attended New York Yearly Meeting—I had several recurring dreams.

I'd find myself enrolled in a college, and it was nearly the end of the semester. I hadn't attended any of my classes, completed or even begun the coursework, nor discovered where my classes met. It was far too late to catch up. My own procrastination had placed me where I was.

In a more disturbing dream, I'd betrayed someone who loved and trusted me, and who would never do what I had done. My act could not be undone, and I knew I would have to confess my deed to the person whose trust I'd broken. Our relationship would never be the same.

I awoke in anguish, which gradually eased into relief as I realized I hadn't done anything wrong. But the distress stayed with me, not only because these dreams recurred—always the same—but also because I never wanted to put myself in that position.

Because of the exact recurrence, almost like a script, along with my feelings in the dream of extreme remorse and a desperate wish to undo what I could not, I worried that I was moving toward such an act without realizing it.

After a few years of this, all the while praying for guidance but still without answers, I experienced an episode in my waking life that brought me closer to God. This series of unforeseen and stressful events showed me that he can use such miserable experiences to help and teach his children. Without this connection, I'd have spent the whole episode spinning my wheels, and probably would have emerged from it in much worse condition than I did.

It began with Cathy's diagnosis. She was only thirty-eight. Talking to Cathy's doctor, my other sister and I gained new information, much of it focused on early detection plus unsettling facts about the disease and how it develops.

I accepted the need for checkups twice a year instead of once, adding a blood test and pelvic ultrasound to my normal exams. The doctors who advised us recommended that I have children as soon as possible and then get my ovaries removed.

When Cathy was diagnosed, I was thirty-two and had been married about six months. Cathy's treatment went well; she went into remission, and I did my best to forget about our scary family history.

About two years later, during a routine ultrasound, one of my ovaries showed up much larger than normal. I was frightened and alarmed until my gynecologist assured me it was almost certainly a benign cyst that would probably disappear. He was right, but this did not reduce my anxiety.

After a few months, I found myself battling chronic dizziness which had begun shortly after the cyst disappeared. My doctor had a good explanation: The cyst likely caused a temporary hormonal imbalance that in turn set off the dizziness. The cyst probably also upset my hypothalamus, the gland that regulates all the hormones in the body, not just those of the female menstrual cycle.

The stress of worrying about cancer could have continued to affect my hypothalamus, hence my ongoing dizziness. We agreed that I just needed to calm down.

Next, I discovered a smooth, walnut-sized lump in my neck. I was reluctant to go to the doctor because the whole ultrasound episode had been, in effect, a false positive, distracting me and creating unnecessary stress.

I knew I was lucky to have my health, but this did not help me escape a tailspin of fear that had been twirling me around ever since the ultrasound. Therefore, the last thing I wanted to do was submit to another medical test and risk another false positive.

But I saw the obvious good sense of early detection for any kind of cancer. This necessity had become more urgent for my sisters and me, since Cathy's cancer had been caught —though by apparent chance—at an earlier stage than Mom's. Hence, her prognosis was much better.

So I had the lump in my neck biopsied. It was negative, and had also begun shrinking. After about three months, it was the size of a small bean.

This should have reassured me, but fear had taken too strong a hold. First the ultrasound, then the dizziness, next the lump; each event kicked the spiral of fear within me into higher gear. That fear overpowered all the good news, credible explanations, and mostly satisfactory resolutions that followed each of these minor problems.

About four months after the ultrasound, my husband, Ellis, and I attended an NFF gathering which included the usual Meetings for Worship in the Name of Jesus. During one such meeting, God showed me that I had lived in fear all my life.

It lurked under all my activities, thoughts,

and decisions. During the previous few years, he had begun to deliver me from this, but the job was not done.

With all that fear swirling around beneath my consciousness, probably exacerbating my current physical symptoms, I could not have hoped to live in the full freedom of which he had given me a taste. Now, he revealed to me, this fear was at last swimming to the surface where I could acknowledge its power to destroy me and become ready to give it up.

Although this brought me hope, I remained anxious about the dizziness—now intermittent—and could also tell I was becoming obsessed with insignificant symptoms. I recalled a small knot I'd always had on the back of my neck; was it bigger than it used to be? I couldn't tell.

Maybe, between checkups, or even before my latest checkup, I had developed ovarian cancer. This was a credible concern, I knew, because Cathy's doctor had explained the ways in which the disease could elude detection, despite the best medical tests. Indeed, Cathy had had no symptoms until the sudden pain that sent her to the emergency room.

I had learned too much, and couldn't keep that knowledge from scaring me. What did the occasional twinge in my pelvic area signify? When I did my daily sit-ups, I tried to figure out if my abdominal area felt normal under the working of those muscles. There were dozens of subtle ways I could notice possible abnormalities.

Sometime during this period, in the few months before my next checkup, my many fears coalesced into a conviction that I had ovarian cancer. I believed the grain of truth in books I'd recently read, by Bernard Seigel and Norman Cousins, that a healthy mind fosters a healthy body. Therefore, what was all that fear doing to me? I didn't like to think about it.

I only wanted to be well and happy, not dizzy; unworried and carefree as I had been before that ultrasound. *If only I'd had that test a month earlier or later*, I lamented to myself, *none of this would have happened. Why did I have to be the victim of a random event? If only I didn't have a family history of ovarian cancer and had never embarked on that early detection regimen.*

More than half-convinced I was going to die young, if not of cancer then of something else, I felt that the real world was closed to me. That bright, happy, healthy world I'd previously occupied lay across a chasm I could not breach.

One day I said to Ellis, "This has gone on long enough. Even though I'm hardly ever dizzy anymore, I'm still afraid—of everything. I'm so afraid that I'm starting to worry that I'll be afraid for the rest of my life. I'm totally self-preoccupied, and I know it. Counting my blessings doesn't work," I continued, "not that it ever did. It just makes me feel guilty to try to be grateful and then fail. But God isn't giving me a sense of my blessings either. I can't pull out any of his past lessons or comforts to make them work for me now. All of that has crumbled to dust. I used to be happy. I want my life back."

"You're not supposed to hold onto your life," Ellis replied. "You're supposed to give it up."

Sure enough, my life belonged to God, for him to handle as he thought best. I found momentary comfort in this reminder that probably I'd be more at peace, now and in the future, if I wished for God's plan ahead of my own. This brief exchange with my husband was a tiny light in the vast darkness that had settled over me in the past five months.

My next semi-annual checkup was only a month away, and I dreaded it. Half-believing I had ovarian cancer, I kept imagining what it would be like to receive the diagnosis. I could see the grave expression on the doctor's face as he broke the news.

I could feel the shock in the pit of my stomach as I realized my life would never be the same again. I knew the rocky way ahead: surgery, chemotherapy, a life overshadowed by illness. Because my mother and sister had faced these things, it seemed all too possible I would share their fate.

A corner of my mind knew I was probably

healthy, and that if my upcoming checkup was normal, this could provide solid evidence that my fears were groundless. But my fear of going to the doctor was equal to my fear of not going. So there I was, paralyzed like a mouse between two hungry cats, my appointment date marching closer.

The day before my appointment, I suddenly felt I couldn't stand another minute of those nagging worries about lumps and gas pains, those lurid pictures of myself as a cancer patient, that suffocating fear. I felt needled to the point of madness.

I knew of no way out; had I seen an escape, I'd have taken it long ago. Then I began to understand why people commit suicide. What do you do if you can't stand it any longer, whatever "it" is?

I realized that indeed I couldn't stand it any longer. Turning to God, my despair complete, I waited before him, knowing that if he did not rescue me, I was truly lost.

But he shed light on my condition, showing me that I stood in a narrow place between two high, immovable rocks. That place was the valley of the shadow of death. Then I knew I was not alone: Jesus was with me, and he was the way out.

I kept my appointment, at which my ovaries were found normal. I don't remember anything about my state of mind during the following month. I think it must have been pure relief.

# Chapter 7
# My battle with fear: God's purpose

At the beginning of the new year, Ellis and I attended another NFF gathering. The group always spent the first evening on introductions, telling a bit about ourselves and our reasons for attending. These recitations were often long and interesting.

One woman began by stating that she had lost her husband to AIDS two years previously, by a contaminated blood transfusion. Breathless and horror-struck, we waited for the inevitable next sentence, "And then I found out that I had AIDS."

I felt an overwhelming sense of tragedy and grief for this innocent person who had been clobbered by a much worse random event than I had been. In a flash, God lifted me out of the miasma of self-preoccupation and hypochondria I'd been wallowing in for almost a year; my eyes were opened, and I saw that I was surrounded by human suffering.

I knew many of the people in that room. One couple had lost a two-year-old child. A close friend of mine, a widow, had nursed her late husband through years of Parkinson's disease. Another woman, near my age, had recently lost her husband. All this was far worse than my temporary loss of calm and equilibrium.

Finally I felt it from the bottom of my heart, how lucky I was to have my health, my husband, and the countless other blessings God had provided. For months I'd been lecturing myself, piling on the guilt: *What's wrong with you? Other people suffer from random events; they get hit by drunk drivers, contract incurable diseases, or lose their spouses.*

However, until God decided it was time to give me the gift of gratitude, I could not manufacture it. All the world suffers. I had suffered. It was unavoidable. My soul vibrated with the intensity of this revelation.

I knew it was from God because it had the power to lift me out of myself—something all my words and self-admonitions couldn't do—and opened my eyes to other people's needs and pain. Then a voice said inside me, "God restored Job, and gave him twice as much as he had before," (Job 42:10) and I knew my recovery had begun.

One month later, my sister announced a recurrence of her cancer. Then I saw the value of the past year's struggles. I had blamed that cycle of fear and vertigo on the timing of my ultrasound. But I knew the cyst had merely uncovered the fear which had been with me all my life.

Cathy's recurrence wasn't going to pull me back into fear for myself because I was on my way out of it. I continued my early detection regimen, knowing that if God was willing, fear of cancer would never again paralyze me the way it had before my last checkup.

However, I was not yet entirely free. I was still afraid of disease in general, and it didn't help that I had recently heard about a high school acquaintance, several years younger than I, who had almost died of colon cancer. *Why not me?* I kept wondering. *My age is obviously no protection.*

Thus hypochondria resurfaced, in worries about twinges and the now tiny lump in my neck. Although these worries didn't have much power, they were a constant small nuisance, like mosquitoes buzzing around and occasionally biting.

After awhile this began to drive me crazy, until I finally saw to the bottom of the early cancer detection trap. The lure of that trap is, If you don't pay attention to this lump or that twinge, *you will die of cancer*, because look what happens when cancer isn't caught early.

Of course early detection saves lives, but obsession with one's health can also ruin a perfectly good life. I saw that I was indeed ruining my life by listening to what passed for common sense: *You might die of cancer if you don't go to the doctor and get that twinge checked out.* Listening to this voice, and always wondering about my health but never going to the doctor, was a prescription for insanity.

It was like being in a small, dingy house with no exit. God showed me that I occupied that house, and that I had several options: Continue to exist in that shrinking space while breathing its deadly air, visit the doctor and submit to a battery of unnecessary, possibly inconclusive tests, or turn my back on all those worries forever.

Although inviting, this prospect was also scary. If I wasn't sufficiently aware of twinges and lumps, might I let something important slip by, and end up dying of cancer before my time, all for lack of attention to my health? My mother, at fifty-four, believed that one of the reasons for her late-stage diagnosis was that she had been "cavalier" about getting annual checkups.

Cathy's case had been different; like our other sister and me, she had been getting a checkup every year, but apparently that had not been enough, given our family history. Although I'd recovered from the shock of her diagnosis, I still saw the undeniable good sense in the six-month checkup schedule we had all adopted since then.

To exit that dingy little house of perpetual worry meant to trust my health to God. But what if he let me down? What if I decided not to worry anymore, paid attention only to my ovarian cancer risk, continued with those tests, and forgot about all other types of cancer? Then what if I died of colon cancer, lymphoma, or breast cancer, because I relinquished my worries about, and therefore my attention to, my health?

Pondering this, I began to see that it might actually be better to die than to live my whole life worried about one fatal disease or another. As things stood, this worry did not propel me to the doctor, nor did it reassure me that I was looking after my health by thinking about it all the time. This state felt like living death. I had endured it for more than a year.

Then I saw that it really was death—a spiritual condition that would eventually kill me through depression, despair, or some other stress-induced illness. When I realized this, I turned to the sensible, logical voice that never stopped pestering me about lumps and twinges and said, "You say I might die if I don't listen to you. Well, I'd rather die than listen to you another minute." It was joy and triumph to see this and to say it. It was my freedom.

All of God's lessons to me during the following year were about liberation from fear. Whenever he helped me face down a major fear, greater freedom followed. When the most expert physician I had yet consulted told me that early detection for ovarian cancer is uncertain at best for a woman of my age, I should have been terrified.

Instead, God put abundant rejoicing into my soul. He showed me what aspects of my health I could control, and gave me lasting peace about the things I could not control.

When Cathy announced her second recurrence and subsequently almost died of complications from an experimental chemotherapy treatment, I felt no fear for myself. When she announced her third recurrence, still I was not afraid. Therefore, I could continue to help her without worrying about myself.

Before this point, I could not have seen the purpose in the misery and self-preoccupation of the previous few years. But now I could see it, and it was irrefutable.

# Chapter 8
# Learning complete obedience

My life was not my own: This was the main lesson of those months of hypochondria and fear. If I could release my whole self to God's care, he would give me the peace I could not manufacture. But my life was not my own in other ways, and this lesson continued during the next few years, culminating in a series of unmistakable visitations.

The first episode, though unspectacular, was revealing. About six months before our first child was born, I commented to Ellis that I couldn't control my bad moods.

"I try so hard," I lamented, "but I get crabby and whiny no matter what I do. It comes and goes, and I can't suppress it, no matter what."

"Are you still reading Time and Newsweek magazines?"

"Sure I am; they're interesting. Why shouldn't I?" It had never occurred to me to restrict my reading, which was well within the bounds of decency.

"You might try stopping, and see what happens."

I knew he was well-seasoned in following the Lord, and therefore probably had a good reason for his recommendation. So I stopped reading *Time* and *Newsweek*. Not long thereafter, I noticed I could better control my bad moods.

This was the beginning of a lesson I needed in my coming task of taking care of young children: I soon discovered I lacked the superhuman patience for the job. I always vowed I would not yell at our children, nor become impatient with them in other ways, but my inevitable lapses taught me that I could not control myself just by deciding to.

Not long before our second child was born—about two years after our first—I had a recurring dream, always unfolding in three stages. In the first, I was traveling with our children. If it was time to stop for a meal, I decided not to eat or to get food for the children. Or, if I found myself at a crossroads, I took the wrong turn. Once, I was in a train station and knew when and where to board the right train. I loitered until it had left.

These opportunities were limited; they arrived, then passed, and when the moment of choice was upon me I knew I'd not have another chance. No wonder I felt a sense of misery and regret during the second stage of these dreams. *Why didn't I feed myself and my babies while I had the chance?* I moaned. The journey was over and not only had I chosen wrong, I'd known it at the time.

In the third stage, I suffocated. Sometimes I was in a close, dark hole. At others I was trapped under a fallen building with my oxygen supply running out. In a few instances I simply felt I couldn't breathe. Death was imminent.

I woke with pounding heart and clammy palms. It was hard to get back to sleep, not only because these ending episodes were so real and so horribly in line with my worst waking phobia, but also because it all felt true.

Nonetheless, I could make no sense of these dreams. As they continued, I became more and more concerned, and began to pray for guidance and insight. Shortly thereafter I saw that I'd erected a substantial barrier between myself and God. Furthermore, I'd done it years ago and known at the time that I was shutting off the Lord.

During that whole period, I'd failed to realize the seriousness of the problem and thus had been blind to its effects. This barrier was a set of terms and conditions I'd laid out a decade ago, as in, "Lord, I'll do anything for you except..."

My list was long. I didn't want to travel as a missionary to Africa or South America. I refused to confront my abusive father. I insisted I'd never act like certain people in my life who had offended me only because they had spoken the truth in obedience to God.

All these conditions were rooted in fear. I was afraid I'd die of a tropical disease, plus I didn't want to place my musical career on hold. I felt I could never oppose my father. I wanted people to like me.

I knew these fears betrayed a lack of trust in God, but I was powerless to change. More, I didn't want to. This attitude held until God connected my recurring dream with these sins.

I saw that the first stage represented my list of conditions and God's call to relinquish it. In the dream, I declined the opportunity, just as I'd been doing in real life.

The second stage represented what would happen, or what was about to happen, if I refused to give up my list: I'd be swallowed up in chagrin and despair over the foolishness of my decision. But unlike in my dream, my chance had not yet expired.

Then I saw the fate which would rest on the resolve to give up my list or not. As with the third stage, I'd suffocate if I chose wrong. Yet if I relinquished all my fears and future actions to God's will, the path of life opened up before me.

The way illuminated by this inner picture was so compelling that it didn't even feel like a choice: I was terrified of suffocating, so it was easy to turn away. My list fell from my grasp like a stone slipping through slack fingers, and I felt boundless gratitude for the clarity of God's word. Peace and a deeper connection with the Lord followed, and from that time on I knew I could count on his inward care and protection.

This was soon tested, because shortly thereafter, I felt a strong nudge to warn my father about his behavior. He was then seventy-four years old. Realizing what God required, I discovered I was no longer afraid to do it, proving the truth of Isaac Penington's statement, "[A]s the soul in faith gives itself up to obey, so the power appears and works the obedience . . . the power never fails the faith." (Benson 1983, 25)

A few years previously, Ellis and I had moved to Casper, and lived about nine blocks away from my father. It was simple to call him and set up a visit. As I'd suspected, when I delivered the message God had given me for him, he refused to listen.

However, I benefited because during the conversation I gained many new insights into his behavior. Ever since high school, more than twenty years ago, I'd emerged from almost every encounter with him frustrated, angry, and bewildered. But this time I saw his twists and dodges, and he couldn't lead me around by the nose.

In addition, over the following months, I discovered that many of my other fears had vanished, including some that had never been connected to my list. Thus, I learned that one of the rewards of walking in the path of life is freedom from fear—an even greater freedom than what I'd already experienced after confronting my fear of cancer.

# Chapter 9
# Learning complete trust

Coinciding with my *Time/Newsweek* struggle, I was grappling with several contradictions at once. I saw that the Bible points to love, healing, and protection for God's people, yet I also knew the world is full of suffering and unchecked evil. More puzzling still, my own life showed clear evidence of God's physical care and protection.

One day I was sitting in our car at a red light on a one-way street. There was a line of traffic in both lanes, and I was on the right in front. The intersecting street was a four-lane thoroughfare, but no traffic was in sight when the signal changed. On the green light I shifted into gear, began to move forward, then hesitated. The driver on my left glanced over at me and paused.

In those three seconds a car shot through the intersection from my side at forty miles per hour or faster. It was clear that the woman at the wheel had no idea she'd run the red light until she was nearly through. It appeared that she was oblivious of the fact that she was even driving.

Her car was big, a predecessor to today's largest SUVs, and our four-door Honda Accord would have been smashed. The car to my left would also have been damaged, as well as those closest in line behind us.

Afterwards I knew it was the hand of God that had held me back. This was one of a series of experiences proving his watchful care. However, on a slightly different front, I had never really believed that God would "give us this day our daily bread." (Matt. 6:11) This was apparently a piece of skepticism I had to get beyond.

The events of the next five years didn't help, because we faced so many adversities that I began to doubt God's outward provision entirely. The episode that shook me most was small, even trivial. Yet it sank me deep into misgiving because Ellis and I had been so committed to preventing it.

We had one credit card which we used as wisely as possible. At first we never made a purchase unless the money was in the bank to pay that bill. Later, because even necessities were becoming too much for our shrinking budget, we began charging essential items based on our projected ability to pay.

   This worked because our earnings, though small, were stable. When a bill arrived we could pay it because we knew our minimum monthly income.

   Then one of my cello students paid late. Because of this we did not collect enough of our month's earnings to pay our credit card bill in full before the due date. Our remaining balance was less than $20, but even a penny was unacceptable to us. Why did God allow this?

   Next, we lost our entire livelihoods due to chemical sensitivities that bar us from working with or for other people, in an age when working remotely was in its infancy. Our rocky climb to earning a living from home so bruised my remaining trust that I worried about money all the time.

   This stage ended in one miserable episode. In May 2007, we had a severe spring snowstorm, the kind that dumps more than a foot of wet snow in twenty-four hours, sinks the temperatures into the low twenties, and kills newborn lambs and calves. Our family was in the midst of a move out of town, to the strawbale house-in-progress Ellis was building at the base of Casper Mountain, about thirteen miles west of Casper.

   We had four walls, a floor, and a roof—and a woodburning stove for heat. Since the storm would almost certainly block access to our new rural property, Ellis and the children decided to spend the few bad-weather days out there, working on the interior of our new house.

I decided to stay at home in town, doing what work I could, and packing our belongings. When our mile of dirt road that led from the paved highway to our property was again passable, I would rejoin Ellis and the children.

Because the trend for the past few years had been toward increased expenses and decreased earnings, I was in a snit at God for allowing this. Thus, I felt he'd left me with no choice but to pit my will against our circumstances.

Since our house in town was heated with a natural gas furnace, we tried not to consume any more fuel than necessary. This was one of the budget cuts forced on us by our tightening finances. Because I was alone that weekend, and didn't have to concern myself with anybody else's comfort, I kept the thermostat as low as I dared.

I only turned it up when I was so chilled that I couldn't stand it another minute. I was even cold overnight. Never admitting to myself that this rigor was likely to save us only five to seven dollars, I didn't think about other possible consequences. We couldn't afford anything, I felt, and so believed I was doing what I must.

About four days later, I discovered my colossal error. I had allowed myself to become so cold, for a period of days, that I became sick shortly after joining my family. Much worse, after recovering from the most obvious symptoms, I remained so fatigued that I had to spend most of my time resting.

I lost months of work and attempted work, at a juncture when our family needed every member to be able-bodied and ready to continue the arduous task of escaping the normal summertime pollutants of lawnmower exhaust, spraying of trees and gardens, as well as mosquito spraying by the city at night, and all the perfume and hair spray residues venting out of people's houses through their now opened windows. Casper was only 50,000 people, but it was too much for us.

Shortly after I discovered that I was probably going to be down for weeks or months, I realized that in the future, trusting the Lord for material as well as spiritual care was my only course. Certain disaster lay in the opposite direction.

There was one good outcome. Our children, Annette and Lewis, were then fourteen and twelve. They had to do most of my work, and one day I was trying to rest on our bed which we'd pushed into a corner of our house, about ten feet away from our improvised kitchen. While they were washing the lunch dishes, I heard Lewis say to his sister, "What would Mama and Daddy do without our help right now?"

# Chapter 10
## The early Quakers and freedom from sin

In 2011, about four years after that May snow-storm debacle, God taught me a major lesson about an important aspect of faith. I'd been wrestling with this question ever since I began reading the Bible and, a few years later, started going to church.

Why did so many Christians believe they were stuck in sin, with no hope of escape as long as they lived? This puzzled me no end because the entire thrust of the Bible is God's call for holiness and righteousness. The story of Noah's Ark is perhaps the best example: Genesis Chapter Six tells how God became grieved at people for their wickedness, and decided to flood the earth to kill them all except righteous Noah and his family.

At church, nobody wanted to talk about a life without sin, or else they opposed any such expectation. George Fox discovered this also: "[O]f all the sects in Christendom (so called) that I discoursed withal, I found none that could bear to be told that any should come to Adam's perfection, into that image of God and righteousness and holiness that Adam was in before he fell, to be so clear and pure without sin, as he was." (Fox 1952, 32)

In attempting to discuss this matter with various other people, I noticed that the effort was nearly always derailed by the question, "Are you claiming to be perfect?" clearly leveled at me, the person who brought the subject up.

Implied in this question are several concerns or agendas, all related but not precisely the same: "I'm not perfect and don't see how I can be." "I don't want to be caught in a claim that I'm perfect and then have to defend it, explain it, or live up to it." "I don't want to be accused of arrogance, nor do I want to be guilty of it."

But these objections, valid as they may seem, never led me, and will never lead anyone else, to a better understanding of what it is to live without sin in this life.

As we have seen, I was learning to listen to Jesus' voice and distinguish it from all the other voices, forces, and drives in my life. During all this time, I wondered what Fox and the early Friends had meant when they preached about living without sin. I knew only the first few steps: that I didn't have to be caught between Jesus' commands in the Bible and my inability to act upon them—and that I had better pay attention to any warning dreams he sent me.

I'd also discovered that he required an open, listening spirit, in which I could receive guidance. When I followed this direction, my mind and soul were more settled, and I could do right more often than before. I was less confused and blown about by useless thoughts and plans; the power of fear and worry were decreased; and obedience only became a struggle when I wanted something he did not intend for me.

Still, I sensed I was a long way from understanding, much less experiencing, that state of freedom from sin so much discussed in the early Quaker literature and so little understood, it seemed, by many modern-day Quakers, with the notable exception of Lewis Benson.

In *Catholic Quakerism*, Benson stresses that listening to God, and hearing from him—a "dialogic" relationship—is our proper condition, the state we are created to live in. This releases us from the rigidity of a written, static moral code, and also from the tyranny of human religious authority. It places us directly in touch with God, with the living person of Christ as our intermediary. (Benson 1983, 16-17)

While these liberations were important milestones for me, I still felt that right behavior was eluding me. Although I'd begun to get glimmers of what Fox and the early Friends had experienced in freedom from sin, I knew I did not see their whole picture.

From 1993 on, however, God accelerated my

understanding, primarily in the form of failures under the stresses of raising our two children starting when Ellis and I were forty-one and thirty-six. With the added pressure of career loss and the resulting hardship, my lapses of patience with Ellis and the children became more noticeable and severe.

As I vowed each time to do better, the lesson I learned, over and over again, was that I couldn't. My will alone would never give me the self-control I needed to be a good wife and mother.

During this time, God was gently moving me along. His most important lesson in these difficult years was that when I listened to him, and performed the tasks he required, his power was there for me in stressful moments. I could deal more patiently with crises large and small.

I also experienced more peace in the face of our worsening financial situation. So I began to see a clear correlation between what I did for God and what he gave me in return.

But since these lessons were as much about protection from worry and fear as they were about patience and self-control, I still didn't feel that I fully understood the early Quaker experience of freedom from sin. I did realize one important thing: God was pushing me toward a perfect vision of peace and trust, and a standard of right behavior, especially toward my immediate family.

I never felt that it was right, allowed, or unavoidable, when I snapped at Ellis or the children, nor when I whined, nor when I became petty or snippy. I always knew that better behavior was somehow possible, and perhaps I knew this because I carried within myself a clear sense of how God expected me to behave and the faith that he would give me the power to live up to this expectation.

All the while, he had an important lesson for me, one unfortunate episode that would teach me more than all my previous years of walking with him had done. Typically for such lessons, it began with my barely noticing the path I'd taken, only afterwards seeing clearly where I'd been headed and why I ended up where I did.

Sin, as defined by the early Friends, is the refusal to listen to God, as well as the wrongdoing that comes from this closing of our ears. Since both my outer and inner worlds were free of any drift toward lying, cheating, stealing, adultery, or any other violations of the Ten Commandments, I didn't realize I could still be listening to the wrong voice.

So, during a three-to-four month period, when I thought I was listening to God, and spending part of each day carrying out his requirements, most often in helping to promote the early Quaker message in some way, I was also reasoning with another voice.

This voice was speaking to me about my

writing career. After discovering my chemical sensitivities, I'd had to quit my profession as a cellist because concert halls saturated with perfume and hair spray had become more than my health could take. In addition, with artificial scents invading the air in every other public place, my options for any other employment were few.

However, I could write from home, and although earning money writing is difficult, working outside my home was impossible. So I was trying to be a writer. Discouragement is part of the process, both because creativity can be baffling, and because for every paid writing opportunity, there are hundreds of good writers vying for it.

Since 2008 I'd been working on a book, and four years later I was feeling daunted not only by the setbacks I'd encountered in the writing, but also by the long odds of ever finding a publisher. Realistic thinking, I felt, required me to take an honest look at my chances and to try to make some sort of practical decision based on that factual assessment.

Yet this was in part specious reasoning, and I knew it. I had to finish this project because I got insomnia every time I thought of abandoning it. So instead of contemplating the idea of quitting, I focused on the undeniable difficulty of getting a publisher.

Assisted by that reasonable-sounding inner voice that was always telling me that my writing had little chance of success, even small success, I began to fix more and more on the nearly certain failure of my book, even supposing I'd be able to finish it. *Why go on, since I'll probably never find a publisher?* I thought. *So many people write books that are never published, and that's quite likely to happen to me.*

These arguments were easy to believe because they were so reasonable. Nobody could deny their truth. For every book that gets published, hundreds or thousands are not.

*Writers who are too optimistic about their prospects take their inevitable failures all the harder*, I thought nearly every day, *and I don't want to be one of them.*

So my attitude ran for months, pulling me down and undermining what little confidence I had in my work, until "realistic" visions of failure filled my head. During this time, I didn't notice any direct effect on my self-control and patience, but it was definitely harder to hear from God.

Then one day, I snapped. Out of the blue, I found myself embroiled in a violent argument with Lewis, then sixteen. He wasn't really being any more contrary than at any other time since the beginning of his adolescence, but everything he said drove me wild. This "argument" became more and more one-sided as he shrank into himself and I continued to attack him, until finally I realized what I was doing and stopped.

Chagrin, bewilderment, and self-recrimination followed as I struggled to understand why I'd lost all self-control. I'd been so sure that in doing the daily jobs I knew God was giving me—and trying to stay open to his other requirements for either action or personal change—I'd been safeguarding myself against those lapses of patience and temper I knew so well from prior years. I'd felt I could count on protection because God had provided it on other occasions, some in the recent past.

However, it didn't take me long to realize I had not been listening to God with my whole heart, but had been giving part of my attention and belief to that discouraging voice. Thus, I learned the hard way, and at Lewis' expense, that sin does not always look like sin. Satan is subtle in his designs, alert to trap the unwary, and I'd walked into one of his snares.

This episode appears to prove that we are in fact stuck in sin, because whose judgment is perfect? Won't we always be prone to errors in discernment such as just described?

But if this is true, why did that hard lesson push me further into the conviction that we need not be Satan's victims? We are not always headed for another miserable episode. I got into trouble by listening to the wrong voice, and half-knew all along that it was not God's voice. Therefore, after it was all over, I realized that we always have the option of listening to the right voice.

# Chapter 11
# Learning more about freedom from sin

In our ever-present option to listen to the right voice, we have continuing access to God's power. Then it's available when we need it most. After I realized that freedom from sin is conditional on listening to the right voice, and that this voice is always speaking to us, I learned another important lesson. This one was again about self-control, but the details were more subtle and significant.

After that regrettable lapse that taught me so much, I dedicated all possible attention to listening to God—with a special plea that he teach me how to ignore the most insidious whisperings of the enemy. Staying as close to God as I could, I began to notice a change in my response to a common human problem: daily annoyances.

Mishaps, the small upsets of our plans, and conflicts with others are part of life. No matter how careful we are, how efficiently we try to work, and how harmonious our relations are with others, eventually something knocks us out of our desired pattern.

This reality had been present all my life in greater or lesser degree, but I became newly aware of it because of increased self-control in the face of assorted minor incidents such as dropping a spoon on my kitchen floor. It annoyed me to have to pause and wash the spoon separately from less dirty dishes.

But the next time I dropped a spoon, instead of feeling the usual jet of annoyance, followed by a loud complaint against my own clumsiness, I just sighed, picked up the spoon and washed it off. It struck me, as a new idea, how insignificant these episodes are, if only we could see this—and how little power they have to push us off balance if we are close to God.

Next, I was working in the kitchen in late afternoon; not a good time of day because I'm always tired and there's lots to do. I was behind in my work, and discovered that a key utensil was encrusted with dried-up bread dough, and had to be soaked before it could be cleaned up.

Thus it was unavailable, and I had no substitute. I wasn't the culprit; hours earlier, another family member had used that utensil—not the one he normally used—and I hadn't realized this and so had expected to find it clean and in the silverware drawer.

The enemy attacks us at our weakest moments, and I could feel the urge to fly into a rage, scold, and generally throw a tantrum. However, helped by the Lord, I saw several things that restrained me.

These episodes, at the moment they burst in our faces, feel huge and therefore unmanageable, although they are most often petty. We might feel entitled to our outbursts, but annoying incidents happen a half-dozen times a day, and God does not intend us to be tripped up by them.

It's better to shrug off the event, large or small, and get on with whatever task was interrupted—just what we can't do in our own strength. However, I was amazed to discover that the more closely I listened to God, and did what he told me to do, the more the power of daily annoyances shriveled and dried into dust.

Some days I began to feel so settled and peaceful, so full of joy and happiness, that I nearly didn't recognize myself. Not that I'd been unhappy before; I'd felt many moments or hours of peace and contentment, a sense that I was right with God, my family, and myself.

But this deeper level of peace felt like a new departure, as though I was finally learning what Jesus meant when he said, "I came that ... [you] might have life, and have it abundantly." (John 10:10) This was definitely correlated with how well I heard the Lord each day, and how attentive I was to the jobs he set me: The more I did in response to his daily leadings, the happier I was.

Annoyances continued to lose their power; I could see myself becoming more and more good-tempered, and then I had the best insight of all. I saw what was behind my former mini-tantrums, and why they were so much diminished and sometimes even gone.

On a given day, if I wasn't in that blessed state of peace and happiness, I was, on some level, slightly stressed. Under this barely noticeable stress, I was prey to those inevitable complaints and whinings precipitated by minor annoyances.

By contrast, when God had led me deep down in my soul to the contentment that felt like my birthright, nothing so small as dropping a spoon on my kitchen floor could upset me. Such episodes barely registered; dealt with and forgotten as soon as they occurred.

Additional insights pushed me to the point where I saw why God requires us to transcend even our smallest misbehaviors—and how he always gives us his power if we have fulfilled his conditions. One episode, small in itself, taught me much.

I was rummaging in our small, cluttered storage area, a 10 x 12 foot loft in a corner of our house. One of the objects I had to move was a large plastic garbage bag stuffed with cornstarch packing peanuts. I was chronically irritated by the presence of that bag because I thought we should be throwing away those peanuts or composting them.

Instead, we'd saved them until we had several garbage bags and buckets full—for packing material when Ellis had to ship a wooden bowl or vase to a customer, and also for house construction and maintenance when he needed filler or stiffener for the natural clay plaster that was our finish coating for outside and inside walls. However, it seemed to me that we'd saved far more than we'd ever use.

When I lifted the bag off the stack of boxes I needed to search through, several peanuts escaped from a gap at the top of the bag and fell down through the cracks between piles of boxes. At that point I discovered that my margin of protection for the day was slim—much slighter than I'd realized and barely enough for self-control.

The unexpected power behind the jet of annoyance I felt as those peanuts disappeared into the cracks nearly overbalanced my spirit. I knew that months later, I'd find that litter on the floor of the loft—another annoyance—and be irritated to find my house so messy. Yet right then, digging down for five peanuts was a twenty-minute job, given the number of boxes I'd have had to shift, and I knew the task was beyond me.

My ire was increased by the evidence that somebody had carelessly overstuffed the bag, so that it was nearly impossible to fasten without the upper edge of the bag slipping out of its twisty-fastener. The culprit? Anyone in our household, including possibly me. That event was too far in the past for any of us to recall.

Unable to control my frustration, I thought, *This is all Ellis' fault. If he hadn't insisted that we keep all these peanuts, I wouldn't have this mess to deal with.*

In reality it was a small mess, and at that moment I only had to refasten the bag more securely and descend the loft with the item I'd climbed up to get. I saw these facts, and something else as well: the faultfinding spirit which thrust my impatience forward, and in turn could have precipitated some kind of verbal complaint. Unpleasantness and temporary division would have resulted, something I always regretted, no matter how minor the episode.

A few days later, I saw why God requires complete self-control, even in the smallest matters. "It's all your fault," an accusation leveled at spouse, children, co-workers, or whoever is handy, doesn't stop with a single incident, nor does it stay under control.

In my case, I saw back through my marriage more than twenty years when our money problems were just beginning. "This is all Ellis' fault" had a much more lethal thrust for our relationship when, in a low moment, I decided to leave him. Fortunately, I saw my mistake in time to avert a separation.

Sin starts in the heart. Blaming others in small things, if not reversed, will inevitably lead to blaming them in more serious matters. Thus Satan attacks us within, gaining his foothold little by little until we have forfeited our self-control.

By contrast, the power of God is always there, brilliant sunshine we can step into at any time to escape the chill shadow of lies and deceit. The path is by hearing and obeying; and not lagging along the way.

As I continued to observe the victory of God's power over the small adversities of life, I noticed that my inner condition of moral frailty never really changed. I could always get upset about the little things, and only the Lord's intervention kept me behaving well.

From this continuing reality, I learned the most important lesson of all. Freedom from sin is not a state at which we ever arrive. We have no special skill to avoid sin, nor can we develop it. We have no inherent ability for righteousness that grows or matures.

There is nothing in our human nature that enables us to progress to a state of infallibility, or even goodness. At the age of eighty, we are just as helpless in this regard as we are when infants. The "potential" for a life without sin isn't in us.

Instead, we must depend on God. Staying as close to him as we know how, we need to realize that our sole hope for good behavior lies in hearing and obeying his voice. Then we are in the only possible state for living the life of complete obedience he intends for us.

# Chapter 12
# Help with my anniversary reactions

In 2013, the year before Annette left home, God delivered me from a major component of the effects of early traumas.

Growing up with an alcoholic father included an adult affliction, "anniversary reactions." These are so labeled because of their annual recurrence. Mine were tied to a series of traumatic events which had begun midsummer, culminating about three months later when my father was arrested in October 1965 for threatening my mother, my sisters, and me with a butcher knife. I was nine years old.

Each year, starting in July, waves of anger, misery, and despair would hit me out of no-where, almost always catching me off guard. I'd be walking on the dirt road near our straw-bale house, enjoying the cool summer breeze of early morning, and suddenly an overpower-ing blow would hit me, as from an invisible sledgehammer.

Paralyzed by this stress, my whole body would seize up, and I seldom made it back to the house without pulling a muscle. Or I'd be working in the kitchen, and darkness would wash over me in an evil tide. For no reason at all, I'd find myself thinking, *Why do I even want to be alive?*

I was emotionally fragile, so that the tiniest mishaps made me want to cry; I felt sad and depressed much of the time; and I moved my body wrong without even realizing what I was doing until I'd half-sprained a wrist or ankle in some simple motion I performed every day. But worst of all was how I treated Ellis and the children.

Often I couldn't anticipate these waves and therefore didn't realize I had to be on guard. In the midst of an attack of anger or despair, I'd find a reason to yell at a family member, or to sharply criticize. At best, I was petty and sullen; at worst, a persecuting shrew.

I came to dread these outbursts, and my only hope was in prior experience with those waves. They eventually subsided, and I could think clearly between them. I also knew that most years I could expect relief starting in late October and lasting to the following July.

However, this wasn't always true. Sometimes, from December through mid-January, black depression would overpower me. Rather than coming in waves, it settled on me, a dark cloud that refused to lift. The first time this happened, starting in about 2010, I suspected that this was my mother's darkness along with my own feelings about the illness that killed her.

When she was diagnosed with late-stage ovarian cancer in November 1982, at fifty-four, she quickly gave up. During her remaining twenty months, I observed her sporadic efforts to help herself, struggling all the while against my father's lack of support. Her illness and death, I felt, were the last and most lethal manifestation of her sick relationship with my father.

Although he'd quit drinking more than thirteen years previously, he still abused her. She lived by "forgive and forget," which I believe was the psychological equivalent of swallowing a poison pill each time. She had no other way to escape him except to die. So at holiday time, my recollection of her self-destructive behavior, plus my unresolved grief about her death, devoured me.

Sometime in 2011, I began to pray that if there could be an end to my anniversary reactions, God would help me through the process as fast as possible. I knew I had to declare myself ready to endure whatever adversities this request might precipitate and so, with no idea what I was facing, I told God to go ahead. Not surprisingly, for the next few years, my summer anniversary reactions started earlier, lasted longer, and were more severe.

Eventually I was struggling with waves of misery most of each year, because the October phase lengthened until it overlapped the December-January phase, which in turn extended to nearly meet up with what had become the late spring-early summer phase. These attacks were so stressful and distracting that after a few years, I forgot for months at a time that this might be the beneficial process I'd declared myself ready for in 2011. Then a calmer state of mind would surface for a short while, and I'd remember.

God did not desert me during this time. A few years previously, throughout the worst of our money problems, I'd learned that if I listened closely to his commands and obeyed his requirements, I could expect some peace of mind —even when homelessness and bankruptcy appeared imminent.

The same help came to me in my anniversary reactions. The more vigilant I was in my general listening and obeying, the less likely it was that a wave of anger or despair would catch me off guard. Thus, as time went on, the problem was almost entirely contained: Although I had no internal defense against my attacks and simply had to wait them out and silently pray for help, the only thing my family knew about it was that I was irritable and gloomy.

In summer 2013, after several years of nearly continuous anniversary reactions, the problem intensified again, but instead of waves that broke and subsided, it became a cyclone of anger in my chest. I had to live with it day and night, the way one lives with a storm that never really stops.

Sometimes the clouds on my soul would thin or break apart and I glimpsed the sun; then darkness would overtake me, and I knew myself to be again under a curse. Would it ever lift? I felt trapped by these attacks, which I could not control. Clearly, the legacy of misery and anger left me by my father was evil, and just as clearly, God was not the author of it.

Even more obvious to me, he had power over it. Therefore, why did he let it go on and on? I felt always on the edge; never safe from the lapses of patience or temper that had so often occurred in the recent past.

All I could do was cling to the Lord, obeying him as best I could, and most of the time he gave me the self-control I was praying for. Yet it was a miserable way to live and, swallowed up in my struggle, I wished only that it would end.

Gradually, however, I realized that God almost certainly had a plan for me and, just as in our worst financial circumstances, I knew I could count on the ultimate good of that plan, even if I couldn't understand why the process had to be so difficult.

Not long after that, I remembered that I'd declared to God, several years previously, my readiness to undergo whatever was necessary to end my anniversary reactions for good. I'd put myself in his hands, not knowing what was next, and now I was finding out. My current ordeal was the answer to my prayer for deliverance, and when I realized that, I began to see other things as well.

First, I realized that the process that was so hard for me could be the exact plan God was using to set me free. Once I saw this, I ceased to resist it or wish it would end.

I understood that God would accomplish his purpose in due time, and my job was to wait. A key feature of this transition was the mastery I gained over my feelings—not mastery over the cyclone, but over my lifelong response to adversity.

"I hate this and wish it would stop," had always been my reaction. I felt that since God had made me a feisty person, one who doesn't often give up, and fights through many difficulties rather than backing away from them, that I was entitled to my feelings.

Besides, I was convinced I should talk to God about my deepest problems and dilemmas, including misery, despair, and a wish that my adversities would end. If I couldn't be honest with him about how I felt—since he knew anyway—what else was I supposed to do with those feelings?

So I'd never questioned the rightness of honestly facing my feelings, but now I began to see that I could also let go of them. How were they helping me in the current situation?

As soon as God showed me that I could let go of my attitude, he also gave me the power to do so. Then I saw the most important thing yet. In addition to his specific plan, God was using my miserable circumstances to help me in some other way I couldn't grasp. My job was to trust him.

This was a notable gain in my understanding of how God uses trials in the life of a believer. Prior to this, I'd known that "God is present with us in our trials," and "God works through our trials," but my concept was limited to a picture of him standing on the far side of a fog bank, or a thorny hedge, speaking to me despite all that interference, and piercing through the obstacles created by the trial.

Now, however, I saw that he was using the cyclone as a tool in his hands to help me. My worst trials could be directly put to work by God as a positive force in my life. As soon as this new idea took hold, the cyclone vanished. One day it was there; the next, it was gone. Better yet, this disappearance felt final.

Weeks passed and I held my breath, hardly daring to believe that this severe trial was over. I'd never doubted the power of God to overcome it; rather, I had so long felt powerless that many times I'd wondered if that cyclone and all my other anniversary reactions were with me for life.

The peace and gratitude I felt in this aftermath were incomparable; my mind was much clearer, and important insights continued. The best of these was the realization that "I hate this and wish it would stop" was a form of resistance. Therefore, it had been getting in my way: If I were paying undue attention to my feelings, how could I be listening with my whole attention to God?

If I'd realized sooner that "being honest about my feelings" was dividing my attention, I'd surely have stopped. He knows best. He knows best, no matter how my circumstances look to me. During prior years, I'd thought I believed this, but the undeniable fruit of my deeper trust in his judgment was the absence of that whirlwind.

Furthermore, my new peace of mind went beyond just the relief and gratitude of my recent release. I'd found a rock to put my foot upon, and knew, or thought I knew, that no future trial, no matter how severe, would have the power to erode my trust.

Apparently, this was a challenge to Satan, because I could almost hear him howling in the outer darkness. He would smash me; he would kill or maim one of my children, or my husband; he would inflict a tragedy so severe that I would reverse my beliefs and conclude that God did not know best and was not holding me in his loving embrace.

I'd faced this temptation before and struggled against it, but this time, it had little power. I was too busy listening to God. I still had other trials, though none as severe as the cyclone, and was listening with all my might to hear what he had to teach me with those difficulties, which were also tools in his hands to help me, just as the cyclone had been. I felt that I'd discovered a fundamental law of my being—although I'd been trying to listen to God for years, this felt like a new departure.

I could trust him absolutely, no matter how bad my life might become to the outward eye. In this blessed state, I could see the love and patience of the Lord: How long had he waited for me to see that I shouldn't let my feelings get in the way of hearing his voice? He had to lead me, step by step, along the path he blazed especially for me, until I saw.

This is a deep lesson that can't be forced or hurried. As we have seen, when my friend Samantha suggested we study the book of James, I ran into the admonition to consider my trials "pure joy." My mother was losing her battle with cancer, and the timing of this Bible study was wrong. It ended badly for me, though God used the episode to lead me back to him.

God must prepare the believer to obey, by the processes he chooses, implemented in his own way and time. Thus, in his hands and his alone, we can learn the most important lessons and from them enjoy the deepest blessings.

(An earlier version of this chapter was presented at an NFF gathering, Casper, Wyoming, July 2015)

# Chapter 13
# Whose approval?

I had another direct encounter with the Lord in 2005, two years before that May snowstorm during which I refused to turn up the heat—knocking myself down for months afterward. By 2005, it had been ten years since that series of clear warning dreams in which I'd dawdled, refused to get food for myself and my children, and missed a train.

This 2005 encounter began with a leading to speak to a friend and colleague; a fellow music teacher in my community whom I liked and respected. Something big was at stake for me, I soon learned.

Weeks before this leading, I'd made an appointment with him to talk about something else. But ten minutes beforehand I saw beyond any doubt what I was really supposed to say: "You are not living a life of obedience to God."

I'll never forget the struggle this command

set off in me. I didn't want to admonish or rebuke my friend, and there was a good chance that such a conversation would end our relationship.

My clash with God was brief and to the point. I could feel myself resisting, and he said, "So you don't want to deliver this message. So you suspect it will be rejected and thus do him no good. So you don't want to lose his friendship. But what about you? What will you lose in your relationship with me if you disobey?"

From those inward words, so clearly spoken, I knew that this command to deliver the message was for my benefit as well as my friend's. Furthermore, I sensed I was at a turning point in my life after which I could expect great blessings if I obeyed, and serious trouble if I refused.

Yet still I fought. Dreading a conversation that was nearly certain to turn out badly, and not wanting to make myself a pariah, I argued. "I don't want to do this," I told him. "Isn't there another way?"

In that moment I saw Jesus standing within me, opening up a path that would take me deep down in my relationship with him, deeper than I'd yet traveled. If I obeyed the Father, I would live at his feet, and suddenly I realized that was where I wanted to be.

The sense of peace was profound. I could feel myself sinking down to a place of shelter and protection in which I knew that from then on it would be easier to hear God's voice than ever before.

As I'd feared, the conversation with my friend was miserable. I told him I had a message from God, and delivered it. He was deeply offended, and it was the end of our relationship.

For me, however, it was the beginning of closer communion with the Lord, which I was soon to need. Over the next few years, our financial reserves melted to nothing and our debts mounted until we had hardly a dollar left for groceries. Our children were growing up amid the chaos and stress of Ellis' and my efforts to create the least toxic living environment, the most nutritious and sustainable diet and, at the same time, to figure out how to earn.

We tried to shield them from the worst of our money problems, but the day came when we had to tell them the truth. We owed $26,000 on our credit card, were staggering under the monthly payments of more than $600, and had been accepting help from private charity.

Annette was then nineteen and attending our local community college on full scholarship and working part-time as well. She disliked the idea of continuing to depend on charity, and in September 2012 persuaded Ellis and me to allow her to support herself, and help support our whole family, out of her summer earnings plus her ten to fifteen hours per week of work during the school year.

This was one of the heaviest crosses Ellis and I ever had to carry, because we'd been committed to financially supporting our children until they earned a bachelor's degree. However, we accepted her offer, since the alternative was possible homelessness and starvation—or at the very least, subsistence farming at our rural property; no electricity, no phone, and no Internet and therefore no way to do business.

During the fifteen months when Annette gave up more than $10,000 of her earnings, cheerfully but with lingering regret, my trust in God underwent a subtle change. Ever since 2009 when we'd reached the end of our meager financial reserves and the limit of our credit, I'd been praying daily, almost hourly, to God to show us the way out.

Both Ellis and I were working overtime to launch careers as freelance writers and to investigate other home-based opportunities as well. For several years we struggled in this direction with little to show for it.

Throughout this period, I knew I was totally dependent on God for my health, energy, and attention, yet still I complained to him, even as I was begging for help and guidance. "Why are you making us go through this, particularly Annette? I don't understand why you won't help Ellis and me earn enough, especially since you have the power to do this, and we would do anything for you."

After months of pleading, with some increase

in our earnings, but still not enough to support us, I began to realize on a new and deeper level that God loved our family and had us in his care, even if I thought he wasn't doing a very good job of it. After all, we weren't yet homeless or starving; both Annette and Lewis were still in college; and we were all in reasonably good health despite the extreme cuts in our food and supplement budget forced on us by circumstance.

Sometime after this began to dawn on me, I saw that God probably had a specific reason for allowing our problems to continue. Annette was still paying a third to one half of our monthly expenses, and Lewis, at eighteen, was forced to purchase necessities, such as snow boots, out of his scholarship funds. I began to be more and more certain that God had not only a purpose, but a plan for our whole family, and that our difficulties would not end until that plan was fulfilled.

Annette left home in June 2014 for a summer internship. In the fall, she was planning to attend the University of Wyoming in Laramie to complete the final two years of her degree. Along with her, we'd decided she would support herself but not us, both because it was time for this change, and we were apparently beginning to pull out of our financial doldrums. However, we had a long way to go.

One August afternoon, I was sitting on the rough deck Ellis had built onto the front of our house. The base of Casper Mountain loomed close in my gaze and above that, the clear summer sky. I was thinking about money.

I told God, "You know that Ellis is sixty-three and I'm fifty-eight. You know we've cut every possible expense. We still aren't earning quite enough, and Ellis' Social Security isn't enough to support us. How much longer can this continue? Please will you give us a retirement nest egg, say $1 million? I'd love to be able to earn that much, and you know I'm willing to work as hard as necessary. Furthermore, I'm sure I have internal obstacles to that kind of success. Please show me what they are so I can overcome them."

The amount of money I named sounded to me like the request of a pampered American, which I knew I was, having been raised in a middle-class family. But I also knew that in the current economy, less might not be enough to generate the dividends to support even our modest expenses.

I'd asked for help overcoming my internal barriers, so I wasn't surprised when I began to feel miserable and confused; this was a clear tearing-down phase. I knew from my recent deliverance from anniversary reactions that it was part of my recovery from early traumas.

A few months later, I was praying for help during an especially strong attack of grief and despair, and saw a clear picture in my mind's eye. I was struggling up a narrow wooden walkway that wound through a steep, rocky canyon. It was desolate and lonely.

I was a tiny figure on that walkway, and could never reach the top. But all at once I became a giant and could leave the canyon with one step. After this, I wanted more than anything else to know God better.

# Chapter 14
# Finding the wisdom of God

After that waking vision of stepping out of the canyon, and my deliverance from anniversary reactions, I was regularly overwhelmed by the wonder of God's sovereignty. He can do anything. I also became convinced that when he withheld something I wanted, or felt I needed, he had a good reason for not granting these wishes.

This led me to see that the wisdom of God was superior to any thoughts and ideas I might have about myself and my life. Whatever I was thinking about—whether a current looming problem; my goals; my frustrations and dissatisfactions; or some aspect of my everyday routine— God probably had the right idea about it, whereas I might or might not.

His wisdom, as applied to my life and attitude, could guide me more quickly and surely to whatever plan he had for me. No matter what lay ahead, I'd be better off going through it with the wisdom of God than without. So I began asking for this gift, and soon realized I was receiving it.

First, I began to more deeply understand "I came that you might have life and have it abundantly." (paraphrase of John 10:10) Over many weeks and months, I discovered that God was unplugging me from trickles of influence from Satan that had been plaguing me for years.

It was as though somewhere in my soul there was a wall of electrical outlets, all with cords plugged into them, leading deep into my consciousness. Tiny but stubborn temptations entered my being via these connecting cords.

The ways in which I noticed that God had yanked these cords fell into two categories: daily or often-recurring episodes, and sudden realizations that my outlook on a major life problem had radically improved. An example of the first occurred when I was setting a digital timer, which I depended on several times a day to remind me to leave my desk, walk around, and roll my shoulders. Or I needed it to waken me from a catnap, or to monitor a cooking project.

This timer, starting to malfunction, often skipped past the hour and minute I was trying to set it for, and then I had to try again until it worked. Ever since this inconvenience had begun, I'd felt a jet of irritation: "Lord, you know we're too broke to replace this stupid timer. It's all your fault we're broke, because you could change that at any time, and enable us to earn more. You know how hard we're working, but you won't help."

However, on a day shortly after I'd asked for the wisdom of God, when the timer skipped, I felt only resigned patience. There was no trace of the usual small but persistent, years-long grievance I'd been nursing about our low income. My snit had disappeared.

Major life problems continued unchanged, and through one of these I discovered the depth to which the wisdom of God had penetrated my attitude. For decades I'd been frustrated about being a writer, even before life forced me to pursue it as a vocation. I've often wished for an easier path.

The primary problem is the same as it was for my first career, cello playing, in which years of work are required, usually far beyond college, before you achieve professional-level skill. Then, establishing yourself and making even a moderate living are as difficult as gaining proficiency was because of fierce competition for few jobs.

Although in music I succeeded in a modest way, my path as an attempted professional writer felt much longer and steeper—all the more because I was in my fifties, not my twenties. So for the past fifteen years, every time I thought about my writing life, it was with increasing frustration.

Long ago, my level of discontent reached a constant whine, despite the beginnings of success which I generally found a way to minimize or dismiss just because not all my efforts were going uniformly well.

These feelings sapped and discouraged me as much as the actual circumstances they were about, and I could count on their recurrence. Somewhere in my soul, there was a blackboard-like surface rolling around and around, and every time it reached a certain point, a fingernail extended, scraping it to cause a screech.

I didn't think about my writing life every day, but sooner or later I found myself wishing I didn't have to work so hard for so little encouragement or material return. After I prayed for the wisdom of God, several weeks passed, as usual, with no particular thoughts about my chronic discouragement.

Then, perhaps a month or more went by before I finally realized that the rolling blackboard, with the fingernail screech that was so familiar, had vanished. That whole dissonant experience had been replaced by a glow of contentment and modest pride at the small successes and steady gains of the previous three years.

Thus, my battle against discouragement, which I'd been fighting for so long, had evaporated. I continued to feel at peace with my path as a writer—a change that only the power and wisdom of God could have accomplished. This had to occur before I achieved any more success, because otherwise I'd probably have at-tributed my new satisfaction to visible gains.

Next, God helped me bypass the sort of snare in my marriage that can trap any couple. Some months before asking for his wisdom, I realized that Ellis and I, at sixty-four and fifty-nine, should put all our affairs in order, beyond merely updating our wills, which we made when our children were minors. There was still plenty to do, from clearing file cabinets of twenty years' worth of obsolete papers to putting as many of our assets into transfer-on-death status as the law allows.

We are do-it-yourselfers and not likely to hire a lawyer for routine work we can learn. There-fore, educating ourselves and dealing with su-perfluous possessions is a big job, one I realized we should begin as soon as possible, while we both have some vigor left.

A few days after I saw this, I mentioned it to Ellis and he agreed that we should get started. Then I asked, "Had any of this occurred to you?"

"No, I can't say that it had."

At similar junctures in the past, I'd launched into accusations, modified and well-disguised, but accusations nonetheless. I'd have thought, and insinuated, *Why did I have to be the one to realize this? Why couldn't you think of it?*

But now this attitude had no opportunity to develop, or even to occur to me, because I saw why Ellis hadn't thought of putting our affairs in order: It wasn't his job. God assigned this particular task to me.

Ellis would help, of course, but I had to initiate it, decide what needed to be done when, and keep the ball rolling. There was a lot of joy in seeing this: the happiness of realizing we could do a service for our children; the knowledge that it was time to get started; and best of all, no faultfinding.

Another important example, this one about periodic trials of the sort we all experience, illustrates the all-pervading character of God's wisdom and how it can change our entire view of our circumstances and help us along, whether our way is rocky or smooth.

One morning, I was facing a cluster of small problems that had landed on me all at once. As usual for these episodes, I had little perspective. Larger problems threatened because of the current minor assault, and I figured it would all culminate in a feeling I'd had every other time, that of struggling to keep my head above water.

This is well described in Richard Adams' novel, *The Plague Dogs*, in which the dog protagonist, Rowf, is fighting to survive in a lab where cruel experiments are performed on the animals. Near the opening of the story, Rowf is desperately swimming; losing strength and hope; about to drown in an experiment tank.

In a similar way, when battling problems large or small, I'd always felt pushed under. Gasping for spiritual air, I'd surface only to sink again into a morass of worry and stress.

However, midway through that recent morning, with its cluster of problems, I realized with the delight and surprise that characterized the timer-setting and my changed attitude toward my writing, that I had no feeling of being in the experiment tank. Instead, I'd been waiting on the Lord as I went about my work, praying for help and—most significant of all—knowing that sooner or later the current batch of problems would end, returning daily life to its usual pattern.

This signal episode, more than all the others, convinced me of the value of God's wisdom. Because I asked for a better state of mind to guide my life, one I can't know, but that is in line with God's plan, I have it. Since then, my burdens have been lighter, and many other problems have dropped out of my consciousness.

# Chapter 15
## The pearl of great value

Blessings from the wisdom of God continued to accrue. More and more often I began to realize the all-encompassing nature of his power, and many times a week, this broke over me with awe and wonder.

Then I saw that since he could do anything—such as fix our financial problems—and so far hadn't, he must have had a good reason. Knowing that his wisdom was superior, I therefore found I was ready to accept present adversities as probably serving his purpose, although I didn't like adversity and never could.

I could also see that God meant to bring me closer to him, so gradually I became more motivated to accept whatever he gave me, as all pushing me in the right direction. In addition, I began to see, or perhaps decided to believe, that every good thing in my life came from God; every bad thing from Satan;

with God making "all things work together for good." (Rom. 8:28)

These insights were clear and powerful. Although I processed them with my reason, they felt like a gift deposited directly into my soul.

After almost two years of discovering the many benefits of God's wisdom, I recalled an episode from two decades ago that he was about to use to further guide me.

Annette was a year and a half old and starting to develop her vocabulary. One evening after we'd put her to bed, I was practicing the cello in our living room just fifteen feet from her bedroom. The door was open.

Every time I paused, her hopeful little voice issued from the darkened room. "More?"

After I'd been practicing about forty-five minutes, and she was still asking for more music, I explained to her that I had to stop and go to bed too.

In a few seconds, she said to herself, "Back," in a settled, contented tone. She knew the cello music would come back, although she'd have to wait for it.

I saw the inner world of a young child: She couldn't imagine losing the cello music. No event had yet suggested to her that good things might not come back.

This absolute security reminded me of Jesus' admonition, "Unless you ... become like children, you will never enter the kingdom of heaven." (Matt. 18:3)

What does this mean? Clearly, we shouldn't abandon our adult responsibilities. And we have to trust God the way children trust their parents.

But in Annette's unshakable knowledge that the music would come back, I saw something deeper. If we really are required to live in that condition, trust has to permeate our being until worry and fear have no more power over us.

However, since all adults have discovered that many things can go wrong, we never lose the memory of the resulting insecurity. This is part of the human condition. Fortunately, God promises hope: "[W]ith God, all things are possible." (Matt. 19:26) and "[B]e of good cheer, I have overcome the world." (John 16:33)

I began praying for the trust I needed and could never manufacture, knowing that God would not refuse me something so important. I noticed no direct result, but did begin thinking more about petitionary prayer. Jesus tells us not to "heap up empty phrases," thinking we will be heard for our many words, because our Father knows what we need before we ask. (Matt. 6:7-8)

The inference is obvious: Don't ask; wait to see what he brings. So I quit asking for things, even when I felt that these needs and wants were legitimate.

Occasionally, this resolve broke down at stressful junctures, for example, in 2017 when Lewis was driving to his college classes on an icy highway in a blinding snowstorm. Then I pleaded for his safety. But the rest of the time I didn't ask for what I wanted, feeling no need.

For two more years, my awe increased at the Lord's sovereign power over both the material and spiritual worlds. My conviction that he is absolutely trustworthy continued to grow. Then, in about 2018, my attitude took another jump.

I realized what I should have requested instead of the retirement nest egg I'd asked for in 2014: $1 million in his coinage. This is the pearl of great value mentioned in Matt. 13:45. "[T]he kingdom of heaven is like a merchant in search of fine pearls, who, on finding one pearl of great value, went and sold all that he had and bought it."

Comparing the material with the spiritual gift, I thought, *A million actual dollars would bring a massive change to anyone's life except a millionaire's. Imagine an internal change of similar magnitude, if God were to give me that much of his power, and all the spiritual blessings that would accrue.*

I wanted this. I'd recently realized that life problems and sources of stress, varying only in frequency and degree, could occur in many forms even if we had enough money. Where would my help come from if I continued to focus on just one difficulty among all the likely ones?

Sure enough, after our money problems abated, other circumstances stressed and distracted us. Some were mild, others severe; all caused me to ask for the Lord's $1 million to get me through.

This desire to seek first his Kingdom held, for the next few years, even under the worst conditions. Though of course I wanted him to deliver us from our trials, I wanted even more to receive the calm and relative peace only he could bring.

He granted it, and so I discovered that the pearl of great value is truly worth all we have. Who among us can banish worry and fear, placing our feet on a solid foundation—present, practical support in bad times as well as good?

# Chapter 16
# The supremacy of God's help

After the Lord terminated my anniversary reactions, I felt I'd received a miracle cure such as those described in the four gospels when Jesus casts out a demon. Despite this gift, my relief was short because I soon began to experience a similar problem.

The same miserable emotions would wash over me, but not tied to any particular time of year. Although this was difficult, the Lord gave me his wisdom, strength, and comfort the whole way through.

First, he showed me the true nature of those feelings. As with anniversary reactions, when a wave of misery hit me, my mind would instantly fasten on a current life problem, large or small, and I'd be briefly convinced it was the cause. This lie, though always tempting, was unsupportable because a devouring sense of despair was clearly out of proportion to a minor mishap such as dropping a spoon on the kitchen floor.

I also began to realize that any bad feelings were out of place in my well-ordered, peaceful, and happy life. Furthermore, I knew I'd been emotionally abused throughout my childhood, and that waves of misery, decades after those events, when it was finally safe for me to experience or remember those feelings, were a much more likely explanation.

Second, the Lord minimized the present effects of those waves. I learned again, as I had with anniversary reactions, that to silently endure, praying for help, was the best way to get to the end of any episode. I knew God was there, helping me to stay outwardly calm no matter how I felt, and that my normal happiness and contentment would return.

Third, he taught me through those terrible feelings. After weeks of daily attacks, important insights would come to me about the lies I'd grown up with and continued to believe, even as an otherwise emotionally healthy adult. Since these lies still ruled a portion of my personality and thinking, they had to be exposed so my recovery could continue.

Fourth, the problem was contained: It was a distraction and a trouble, nothing more. Like bad weather, it came and went.

As time passed, I began to realize how much worse it would have been without the presence and power of God. How could I have gotten through it at all without him, much less weathered it with as little stress as possible?

Having realized this, I saw the full value of the decision I'd made in 2005 to sit at the feet of Christ, just before that difficult conversation with my former friend and colleague. If I'd decided not to risk offending my friend, that would have been a choice against God and for the approval and companionship of human beings. However, no human being can equal God's help, wisdom, and support.

So if I'd been depending on other people at any stage of my struggle, none of the likely outcomes would have been good. Without the wisdom of God, I might have failed to recognize the true nature of the problem for months or even years. I might have believed the lie that my feelings were a reaction to current adversities.

In addition, worse than just minor kitchen accidents, the actions of my loved ones also appeared to trigger these internal attacks—when those actions had nothing to do with my current wave of misery—and the battle to treat my family right would have been much harder.

Reliance on my friends would have burdened and confused them. With no hope of escaping my feelings, I'd have thrashed around, always needing to talk to someone and never gaining much relief.

Since the problem regularly recurred, dependence on friends or sympathetic relatives would have continued far beyond the point where they had time to listen. Plus it's unlikely that anyone could have offered lasting help or insight.

Even if I'd begun to suspect I had a problem entirely separate from my current circumstances, consulting a mental health professional felt impossible: too expensive and time-consuming when I had no time and we had no money to spare, and with no guarantee that it would have helped me deal sufficiently with the assault. Furthermore, I would not take psychiatric drugs or tranquilizers.

Thus, I saw the contrast between God's help and the limited availability and wisdom of any person, no matter how sensitive, sympathetic, or skilled. In 2005, when the Lord confronted me with that choice between a deeper relationship with him and retaining the good will of my friend, only he knew what lay ahead. His loving care, and not my knowledge of the future, guided me toward the help I needed in the coming years.

# Chapter 17
# A lesson about discernment

In early summer 2014, shortly after God ended my anniversary reactions, he taught me a direct contradiction to the arguments that elevate human weakness above the power of God. For years I'd been attempting to describe to professing Christians the early Quaker experience that God can destroy our disobedience.

These conversations always ended the same way. I'd present the undeniable truth that God's teaching and guidance are infallible. They agreed, but added, "Since hearing God requires our human discernment, that will always fail."

How could I refute that? For years I couldn't, until God showed me the answer. The incident began with my going astray, ever so slightly—less than I could immediately detect. I was facing two recent, unrelated, and ongoing encounters with other people, where I'd been right in what I'd said and done.

In one case, I'd called a state office and requested basic information to which any citizen is entitled. The people at that office had stonewalled me, acting paranoid and suspicious; nearly refusing to supply the information.

Puzzled because all the other state employees I'd dealt with were courteous and helpful, I saw no harm in pondering this strange behavior. I pictured myself calling the manager to ask why she'd fostered an office culture so hostile to the public she'd been elected to serve.

The second situation appeared equally clear at the time. It seemed all right to think about who was to blame, and about the possibility of bringing it up—even though this wouldn't have solved anything.

For a few weeks, I pursued these two hypothetical actions and then God sent me a dream. In it, someone was "schmoozing" me, and had nearly led me to the point of serious wrongdoing. At the last moment, I realized what I was about to do.

I announced to the person I'd been following down this path, "I'm stopping. You can get angry at me; you can kill me; you can imprison me; but you can't make me continue. Goodbye."

I tried to get out of the house, rummaging in closets for my jacket, all the while surrounded by a crowd of people, chatting, holding martini glasses, and taking snacks off proffered trays. It was clear that I was the only one interested in getting out.

As in one of Dutch graphic artist M.C. Escher's most compelling lithographs, *Relativity*, two groups of people occupy the same house, but can never be aware of each others' existence because they live and walk on different geometric planes. Some inhabit the "floor," others, the "walls."

On awakening, I realized that God was warning me. It took only a few minutes' thought and prayer to realize which two situations that dream was almost certainly about. I needed no discernment for this, both because God's message had been so clear, and because before having the dream I'd already known, deep down, that I probably shouldn't have been pursuing my two lines of thought.

There was a stern quality about this encounter, but it was also comforting. Clearly, if I continued to listen, he would guide my steps before wrongdoing progressed to action. The warning had been easy for me to understand because it was so very clear, and I realized that probably it had been so clear because I'd been listening to God and praying for guidance all the time.

I also knew that if I wanted such unambiguous guidance to continue, I'd have to accept any future encounters without useless speculations such as, "What if this dream only came from my subconscious?" Thus I learned that his guidance can overpower the deficiencies in our discernment.

# Chapter 18
## Receiving a miracle

Wonder at the power and authority of God continued to break over me at regular intervals. The more I realized that he can do anything—absolutely anything—and in his wisdom chooses what he sees fit, the readier I became to accept the required wait for what I wanted.

So often I couldn't understand why he was withholding something I thought necessary, such as a comfortable financial margin, or permanent relief from my traumatic memories. But I continued to believe that he really did know best.

I accepted, though not happily, the ongoing distraction of miserable feelings. I also began to wonder what they were: flashbacks, a mild case of Post-Traumatic Stress Disorder, or just general fallout from decades-old events? The longer it went on, the more I wondered, until I began to notice that many of these waves and their accompanying feelings were identical.

For example, in the midst of an especially severe attack, I'd begin to feel so awful that I wanted to die. At the same time, remembering that this wish had no cause in my present life, I knew—as one stumbling through a thorny wilderness in a dense fog—that this was a long-ago memory of my reaction to severe abuse.

Nevertheless, this despair also expressed itself in verbal thoughts: *I wish I were dead, dead, dead. I should never have been born.* This response never varied, as though I had only one memory playing itself in my psyche like a broken record.

This didn't match well with my hypothesis of flashbacks or reactions to specific events. I also began to notice occasional different attacks, each with a distinctive feeling, single mood, and thoughts. Although surfacing much less often, when they hit they were as strong as the predominant one.

As I was discovering this, I was also reading *The Myth of Sanity* by Martha Stout, in which she describes what she has learned about trauma from decades of psychiatric practice. After I had read in this book many case histories of people who struggled with varying degrees of emotional pain and associated behavior they couldn't control—almost all originating in severe early traumas—I began to recognize some of these experiences.

In particular, features of Dissociative Personality Disorder, formerly called Multiple Personality Disorder, resembled the separate feelings and moods in my head. They were so distinct from each other, like well-delineated characters in a novel, that one couldn't be confused with another. Furthermore, none could be mistaken for the person I knew was "me."

I'd never had a severe case of this. Although I could detect three fractured-off parts of myself, none ever "popped out" or "took over" in the midst of a conversation with anyone else. Instead, the inside of my head was noisy and disturbing, inhabited as it seemed to be by a strong force that wanted to die; another that despised me, insisting I deserved to die; and a rarely appearing third that snarled to defend me, like a savage dog on a chain.

As with anniversary reactions, this was unpleasant and distracting. However, I could feel God helping me through it by generally limiting my behavior to glum or whiny moods that fluctuated with the intensity of my internal attacks.

But this time I trusted God more; therefore, in all but the worst attacks, I knew he was with me and that the current assault would eventually stop. More important, I acknowledged that he was controlling the entire process.

People enter therapy or mental hospitals for similar problems, and I saw the world's solution. However, I also realized that if I needed a "therapist," God knew every detail of my past, including the exact events that had caused me to wall off parts of myself.

He knew everything that was stewing in my unconscious, and could help me endure whatever temporary anguish likely to engulf me during my recovery. Most significant, I knew he could heal me completely and at any time. Therefore, my path was clear: to await deliverance, and face what he required.

Although the clamor and divisions in my head continued unpleasant and distracting, I knew God would act eventually. I assumed any healing would be gradual; a step-by-step process perhaps similar in some ways to what people call therapy, but in greater depth and including insights only he could provide.

But that's not how it happened. One night, I went to bed under the usual onslaught of conflicting, miserable voices that was normal for that stage of the day.

Then God spoke. "So you want to be rid of this problem for once and for all. Therefore, turn your entire self over to me [something I thought I'd already done many times]: the bad and the good; your worries, fears, gripes, annoyances, whines, grievances; and also your wishes, dreams, hopes, ambitions, and everything else you cherish."

This was easy, because I knew that everything I valued was safe with him. He'd give it back, and I didn't want the rest.

The next moment, I felt his power lifting it all out of me, including my fractured personalities, which he set on a high shelf in a closet in a remote corner of my being. There, they became lifeless wooden puppets, and this change felt permanent.

# Chapter 19
# Who knows the most?

As though this were not enough to propel me out into the streets, grabbing people by the shoulders to say, "Listen to what the Lord could do for you," he gave me two more important lessons within the next seven months.

These apparently began a few weeks after the miracle cure, when God addressed me: "Becky, you already know that your unconscious is still filled with traumatic memories. You've realized you don't want to continue sitting on these volcanoes. They have to blow into the open sometime. However, I could lift it all away from you in a few minutes, just like I did with your split-off personalities."

It was tempting. No more onslaughts of misery and despair; a peaceful psyche, unmarred by the past. Yet I knew that in losing all those difficult feelings, I'd forfeit all future access to memories that could help me make sense of my childhood. I didn't hesitate long, deciding I'd rather have the information, even if the path to it would be unpleasant.

My inner life soon settled into a pattern of fierce assaults, differing from all previous ones in three important ways. They were nearly intolerable in their intensity, lasted much less time, and always resolved into a valuable insight.

Although many were about my past experience and present recovery, over time they changed in character to revelations about God's work in human life. Thus, I discovered I was attending classes and doing coursework in the curriculum I'd enrolled in thirty-five years ago when I'd seen that the power of God is the answer to all human problems. This vision had compelled me to share it—my life assignment.

Those warning dreams from so long ago were true, when God told me, "You've signed up for these classes and let the whole semester pass without even bothering to read the syllabus or find out where your classes met. Now it's final exam week, and you can never catch up in time."

I had to listen to God and obey him unconditionally. This was the coursework for which I had been dragging my feet. He had important things to teach me, and my opportunity to learn and communicate them to others was limited.

I had to complete his requirements before the deadline. No wonder those warnings always culminated in, "If you miss that deadline, you will be so very sorry, and it is an act you can never undo."

However, because of these dire warnings I did eventually begin to listen with all my heart, soul, and strength—although it took me ten years to reach this beginning. Then, before I mastered my final assignments, I had to spend another quarter century in the Lord's school to get to the most recent lessons.

For years I puzzled over an Isaac Penington quote I found in Lewis Benson's *Catholic Quakerism*: "[A]s for your speaking of free will, ye do not know what you speak of: for the will with the freedom of it either stands in the image and power of him that made it or in a contrary image and power. . . . [T]here is no middle state between both, wherein the will stands of itself and is free to both equally." (Benson 1983, 33)

Intuitively, I felt this was true, plus long ago God had shown me my condition if I were on the wrong side of the line between obedience and disobedience. Jesus' statement, "He who is not with me is against me" (Matt. 12:30) further supports this. It seems irrefutable that those not working for God are working for Satan.

But I know and have known many good atheists. These people live by their convictions and are generous, considerate, and courageous. How can they be classed with Hitler? For years, I could only make sense of Penington's denial of a third, neutral state by pondering what God had taught me long ago—that if I were an inch over the wrong side of the line, I might as well have been a thousand miles over it.

I reasoned that this lesson must have been about my internal condition, not my outward behavior, because clearly there's a huge difference between stealing a penny and stealing $1 million—particularly for the victim. I couldn't see how good people could be servants of Satan.

Yet I had observed how they could be his prey. For example, I'd noticed that among those who wanted to be financially generous, some were anxious about money, and this impeded their efforts.

And, as we have seen, I'd learned that despite my strongest resolves, I couldn't always treat Ellis and our children with justice and consideration. I had to depend entirely on God before I could be a good wife and mother.

After those twenty-five years had passed, and I'd consented to keep my unpleasant memories, I was enduring one fierce attack after another. Then God delivered his first important lesson.

It was rooted in a decision I'd made in 2000, to separate from my abusive father, then eighty. I'd learned to maneuver around his worst behavior, but it didn't really work, and certainly failed to protect Lewis, whose existence my father appeared to resent from the day he was born, in 1995.

I felt driven to disown him, the only choice I saw for how to protect myself and Lewis. In addition, as I came to see, his habit of playing favorites with Annette was probably bad for her too. The situation had become unlivable.

I was headed for stress-related health problems if I continued to associate with my father, and found I could no longer travel in that direction. Nor had he shown any sign of changing.

I knew it was a permanent separation. I would not come to him on his deathbed, nor attend his funeral. No member of my extended family, nor friend of the family, nor any of his wide circle of admiring Alcoholics Anonymous sponsorees would ever suspect he was an abuser.

Thus, I knew that in varying degrees I would face condemnation, or sincere, well-meaning attempts to reconcile me with my father and, at best, puzzled silence—the latter from relatives who would give me the benefit of the doubt but had only seen my father's public face, that of a normal person.

To some non-family members, he had even presented himself as a near-saint, a holy man-about-town, generous and caring, talking constantly about God and how important it was for the servants of God to serve others. Although almost everyone knew he'd been an alcoholic, nobody dreamed he'd continued to abuse my mother after he stopped drinking—at the same time talking about how important it is to be a servant.

So a handful of people tried to push me back

into a relationship with my father. Their actions spoke for many more who felt as strongly. One particular relative, who cared the most, tried the hardest. This was all a clear case of good intentions gone wrong.

If not for God's sustaining power during this time, I couldn't have withstood this pressure. Either the stress of trying to resist these people, or of resuming a relationship with my father, would have crushed me.

Through this situation, I began to see the evil power of good people's sincere good intentions. Not one of those who attempted to reconcile me with my father intended to hurt me. On the contrary, they were trying to right what they believed was a tragic misunderstanding.

But because they did not consult God, their own conclusions were their only guide. They couldn't see the truth nor even suspect it. Therefore, they acted on a lie.

How can this be anything but listening to the wrong voice and pushing in the wrong direction? Jesus said, "Thus you will know them by their fruits." (Matt. 7:20) Not by their well-meaning actions, and not by their love for all parties. Not by their conviction that they are working for good.

Rather, by the ultimate good or evil of their efforts. Inflicting damage on others is apparently one of the hazards of the human condition, as is the blindness that comes from ignoring God.

The next lesson, related to this situation, felt

even more important. As I began to think about the impossible position I'd have occupied outside the protecting power of God, I saw that a continued relationship with my father had been a tremendous negative force.

Had I stayed in his reach, eventually he would have annihilated me, though my body might have survived my spirit by months or possibly a few years. Ultimately, the situation would have threatened my life.

In a flash of insight, God showed me that this was the death he'd been warning me away from in 1995, in those uncompromising "give up your list now" dreams and waking visions. A lethal event loomed a mere five years ahead. I could only survive it by submitting completely to his power and authority.

In this I was like a young toddler. After learning to crawl, babies grab any available object, pull up, and start walking around. To steady themselves they reach for whatever they can, not knowing the difference between an upholstered chair and a red-hot metal rod. Good parents foresee these dangers and protect their children accordingly.

God knew my future. Blind to the coming event, I didn't even realize I was going to need his guidance and protection. He knew I would not get through it without full access to his help and so, spelled it out.

Thus, I saw much deeper into Jesus' exhortation to become like little children. (Matt. 18:3)

Clearly it also means, "You must realize that in your level of dependence on your heavenly Father, you are like a little child."

Many people want certain guidance and protection. So they consult fortune tellers, horoscopes, Ouija boards, tarot cards, and other sorceries. But the gift of reliable help in an insecure world is the birthright of God's children, as long as we acknowledge that he knows all and, by comparison, we know little or nothing. Our job is to listen and obey.

# Chapter 20
## "It is not a sin to be tempted."

Some months after discovering I was like a young toddler in relation to what God knows about my life and future, he gave me another valuable insight.

It began with yet another horrible memory, an attack so stressful that I could only lie down under it and await help. In the midst of it, I saw—as I had many times before—that I couldn't have controlled what happened to me as a young child.

Therefore, I couldn't control these attacks; not their onset, intensity, length, or ferocity. Most of all, I couldn't control the anger and frustration I'd felt because of the injustices done to me at the time they occurred, much less control these same emotions in my current life when they surfaced as memories. Nonetheless, God's power held, and they stayed inside me, not troubling anyone else in our household.

   This all prepared me for the most important revelation from God, for me and for the whole world: We are not to blame for our natural reactions to injustice and other wrongs. Our emotions hit us on the instant, allowing us no opportunity to choose what we feel. This is the human condition, and not a sin.

   Sin begins when we refuse to listen to God and to learn from him. When we do listen, we see that uncontrollable emotions lead to uncontrollable behavior.

   This is Jesus' message in Matthew Chapter Five: If we nurse within ourselves the beginnings of adultery, murder, etc., we have already started on the path of outward wrongdoing. "But I say to you that every one who looks at a woman lustfully has already committed adultery with her in his heart." (Matt. 5:27)

   Thus, while we are not responsible for the encounters and events that tempt us, nor for the initial feelings they cause, we are culpable if we fail to acknowledge the power these feelings have over us and our resulting dependence on God.

   In the moment it took me to realize this, God lifted out all the potentially dangerous emotions in this attack and flung them into the air. There they disintegrated into snowflakes, fell, and melted. This was glorious, but I knew I probably couldn't count on it for the future because it felt more like a promise than a settled state.

These were the deep lessons and mysteries of asking for the insights I'd have forfeited by choosing the easier path. Often, because the process was so difficult, I'd regretted my decision, but this attitude was temporary because of the overpowering importance of so much God was teaching me.

However, despite these and many other significant realizations, it all began to feel endless. I'd had enough of attacks and the resulting stress, distraction and often, lost sleep. In the past, as with anniversary reactions, I'd found the courage to ask for it to end, and to be willing to endure whatever difficult events were ahead.

But this time I was sixty-four, not fifty-seven as I'd been in 2013. Stress would take a heavier toll, which I couldn't face. However, I was highly motivated to be done with this process if possible, and decided to leave the decision up to the Lord. He knew how much my body could stand, and I knew he would take care of me. So as usual, not knowing what was ahead, I went on.

# Chapter 21
# Deliverance

Within a few days, life settled into a pattern of fierce, unremitting assaults that kept me awake most or all of the night. This happened every third night; on the other two, I slept. Because of extreme sleep deprivation, I couldn't function well one day out of three. On these days, I had to accept being a liability to my household; indeed, I felt fortunate that I could do anything at all.

During this period, I fell off the pinnacle God had placed me on after ending my anniversary reactions. I no longer believed my trials were a tool in his hands to help me; I hated what I was going through, was sorry I'd asked for the more difficult path, and wished it would end.

The Lord sustained me all during this time, helping and teaching me, even when he wasn't granting me sleep. Nonetheless, it was one of one of the most difficult periods in my recent memory. This lasted about five months.

Then, for no reason I knew of, my nights became much easier, but unpleasant memories from long ago continued to disturb my sleep somewhat. This lasted about seven months. Near the end of that time, I began to hope that each episode was taking me nearer to the last, although I couldn't see further ahead than the next attack.

Thus, except for God's continuing help, I felt I was fumbling in near-total darkness. I had also recently seen that a major miracle would be needed to liberate me.

One night, when I was having a harder time falling asleep than usual, I felt God taking me back to the beginning of my life, probably my conception. It was a long journey down to my subconscious, where I saw a phenomenon I'd experienced many times before. It was so distinctive that I'd named it the White Dwarf, which is a star so dense that a teaspoon, if set on the floor of a house, would crash through to the basement.

This overpowering sense of death had rolled over onto me many times, especially during my adolescence, but also later in my life. All I could do was wait until it lifted and, when I was younger —since I didn't yet know the Lord—avoid doing what brought it on.

The night God took me back to the presence of the White Dwarf crushing me from the beginning of my life, this kept me awake until he intervened. Uprooting all that darkness, he spread it out into a much thinner, wider surface, like a mat on which I could lie down and rest. So I fell back asleep.

Later that night, God woke me up and asked, "Are you ready for me to take this all away forever?" Worried about losing the rest of the night's sleep, I hesitated, but he interrupted me with the same question. Praying for the trust I knew I needed, I assented.

Next, just as when he healed me of my split personalities, he told me to pile everything on the mat: all my traumatic memories, my hopes, fears, worries, dreams, goals, ambitions, desires, plus everything bad in me; it all had to go. As before, I knew I was risking nothing.

He lifted it all away, and since then I have never had another traumatic memory. That stage of my life is over, praise be to the Lord of the Universe and the Ruler of the World, in whom all power and authority rests.

# Appendix

# George Fox's Commission

I was sent to turn people from darkness to the light, that they might receive Christ Jesus; for to as many as should receive him in his light, I saw he would give power to become the sons of God; which I had obtained by receiving Christ. I was to direct people to the spirit, that gave forth the scriptures, by which they might be led into all truth, and so up to Christ and God, as those had been who gave them forth. I was to turn them to the grace of God, and to the truth in the heart, which came by Jesus; that by this grace they might be taught, which would bring them salvation, that their hearts might be established by it, their words might be seasoned, and all might come to know their salvation nigh. For I saw that Christ had died for all men, was a propitiation for all, and had enlightened all men and woman [women] with his divine and sav-

ing light; and that none could be true believers, but those that believed in it. I saw that
the grace of God, which brings salvation, had
appeared to all men, and that the manifestation of the spirit of God was given to every
man, to profit withal. These things I did not
see, by the help of man, nor by the letter,
though they are written in the letter; but I
saw them in the light of the Lord Jesus Christ,
and by his immediate spirit and power, as did
the holy men of God by whom the holy scriptures were written. Yet I had no slight esteem
of the holy scriptures, they were very pre-
cious to me; for I was in that spirit by which
they were given forth; and what the Lord
opened in me, I afterwards found was agree-
able to them. I could speak much of these
things, and many volumes might be written;
but all would prove too short to set forth the
infinite love, wisdom, and power of God, in
preparing, fitting, and furnishing me for the
service he had appointed me to; letting me
see the depths of satan, on the one hand,
and opening to me, on the other hand, the divine mysteries of his own everlasting kingdom.

When the Lord God and his son Jesus Christ
sent me forth into the world to preach his everlasting gospel and kingdom, I was glad that
I was commanded to turn people to that inward light, spirit, and grace, by which all might
know their salvation and their way to God;

even that divine spirit which would lead them into all truth, and which I infallibly knew would never deceive any.

But with and by this divine power and spirit of God, and the light of Jesus, I was to bring people off from all their own ways, to Christ the new and living way; from their churches, which men had made and gathered, to the church in God, the general assembly written in heaven, and off from the world's teachers made by men, to learn of Christ, who is the way, the truth, and the life, of whom the Father said, 'This is my beloved son, hear ye him;' and off from all the world's worships, to know the spirit of truth in the inward parts, and to be led thereby, that in it they might worship the Father of spirits, who seeks such to worship him; which spirit they that worshipped not in, knew not what they worshipped. I was to bring people off from all the world's religions, which are in vain; that they might know the pure religion, might visit the fatherless, the widows, and the strangers, and keep themselves from the spots of the world: then there would not be so many beggars; the sight of whom often grieved my heart, as it denoted so much hardheartedness amongst those that professed the name of Christ. I was to bring them off from all the world's fellowships, prayings, and singings, which stood in forms without power, that their fellowship might be in the holy ghost, the eternal spirit of God; that they might pray in the holy ghost, sing in the spirit, and with the grace that comes by Jesus; making melody in their hearts to the Lord, who hath sent his beloved son to be their saviour, caused his heavenly sun to shine upon all the world, and through them all; and his heavenly rain to fall upon the just and the unjust, (as his outward rain doth fall, and his outward sun doth shine on all,) which is God's unspeakable love to the world. I was to bring people off from Jewish ceremonies, from heathenish fables, from men's inventions and windy doctrines, by which they blowed the people about, this way and the other way, from sect to sect; and from all their beggarly rudiments, with their schools and colleges, for making ministers of Christ, who are indeed ministers of their own making, but not of Christ's; and from all their images, crosses, and sprinkling of infants, with all their holy-days, (so called,) and all their vain traditions, which they had got up since the apostles' days, which the Lord's power was against. In the dread and authority thereof was I moved to declare against them all, and against all that preached and not freely, as being such who had not received freely from Christ. (Fox 1952, Vol. I, 90-91)

# Acknowledgments

My family has contributed enormously to the growth and development of this project. Ellis, in so many of our conversations, has provided wise, pithy advice. As my in-house computer angel, he has bailed me out of countless difficulties, and is my walking concordance for the works of George Fox and the Bible. Our children, Annette and Lewis—also my computer angels—have eased my transition into the digital age. All three have put up with the inevitable consequences of book-writing: distracted attention and household clutter. For support and encouragement, I owe my family all.

Special thanks to Karen Bobonich, who read and critiqued a late version of the manuscript, and to Henry Jason for explaining some key Scriptural concepts.

# About the author

Rebecca Hein, an assistant editor of WyoHistory.org, has been active in the New Foundation Fellowship since 1985. She lives with her husband, Ellis, near Casper, Wyoming.

# Bibliography

Benson, Lewis. *Catholic Quakerism*. Philadelphia: Friends Book Store, 1983.

Fox, George. *Journal of George Fox*. Revised Edition by John L. Nickalls. Epilogue by Henry J. Cadbury. Introduction by Geoffrey Nutall. London: Religious Society of Friends, 1952.

Fox, George. *The Works of George Fox*. 8 vols. 1706. Reprinted, New York: Isaac T. Hopper, 1831. Philadelphia: Marcus T. C. Gould, 1831. New York: AMS Press, 1975.

# Index


adversity(ies), 52, 71, 75, 78, 99, 107

Benson, Lewis, 14, 21-25, 49, 59, 121

Bible, 5, 6, 11, 18, 19, 51, 57, 58, 81

Christ, Jesus, 4, 6, 7, 9, 12, 13, 18-20, 22-24, 31, 34, 38, 58, 59, 67, 84, 100, 101, 105, 107, 121, 124, 125, 128, 135-138

church(es), churchgoers, 2, 10, 14, 17-23, 25, 57, 137

dark(ness), 4, 12, 13, 19, 26, 37, 74, 75, 77, 80, 132, 133, 135

death, 26, 38, 43, 47, 125, 132

discernment, 64, 109, 111

Dwarf, White, 132

fault(finding), 70, 92, 96

fear(s), 1, 34-36, 38, 41, 43-45, 48-50, 59, 60, 101, 103, 116, 133

Fellowship, New Foundation, NFF, 14, 23-25, 34, 39,

Fox, George, 14, 17-

19, 21-23, 57-59, 135

frailty, moral, 71

Friends

    early, 14, 24, 25, 31, 58-61, 109

    Religious Society of, 9, 14, 17, 21, 23

God

    authority of, 23, 113, 125, 133, 138

    blessings from, 40, 68, 81, 84, 99, 102

    comfort from, 15, 37, 105, 111

    dependence on, 71, 86, 122, 126, 128

    dreams from, 3, 4, 6, 31, 32, 46-48, 59, 83, 110, 111, 120, 125

    encounters with, 20, 22, 24, 83, 111

    existence of, 2-4

    guidance of, 9,

God, continued

    14, 25, 47, 59, 91, 97, 100, 108, 109, 111, 125

    healing from, 12, 51, 116, 133

    hearing from, 9, 18, 59, 63, 67, 71, 72, 81, 85, 109, 137

    help from, 29, 32, 43, 67, 75, 76, 79, 81, 95-97, 102, 106-108, 115, 116, 125-127, 131, 132

    lessons from, see teaching of

    listening to, 23, 25, 26, 58-61, 64, 65, 67, 76, 80, 81, 111, 120, 121, 126, 128

    miracles from, 105, 116, 117, 119, 132, 133

    obedience to, 21, 22, 48, 49, 59, 71, 72, 76, 77, 81, 83, 84, 109,

God, continued
120, 121, 126
power of, 6, 12, 15, 22, 25, 27, 29, 40, 49, 60, 61, 65, 68, 71, 77, 79, 94, 99, 100, 102, 106, 109, 111, 113, 116, 120, 121, 124, 125, 133, 135-138
protection of, 49, 51, 60, 64, 69, 84, 125
revelations from, 35, 40, 120, 128
sovereignty of, 91, 102
teaching of, 9, 18, 23, 25, 32, 43, 45, 46, 60, 61, 64, 65, 71, 81, 109, 119-122, 124, 129, 131
trust in, 43, 45, 48, 53, 55, 60, 79-81, 86, 101, 102, 115, 133
visions from, 6, 91, 120, 125

God, continued
visitations from, 25, 45
voice of, 6, 11, 18, 21, 22, 25, 40, 58, 64, 65, 72, 81, 85
warnings from, 26, 59, 83, 111, 120, 121, 125
wisdom of, 91-97, 99, 100, 105, 107, 113, 136
gratitude, 13, 40, 49, 80
heaven, kingdom of, 100, 102, 103, 137
life, 26, 48, 50, 67, 92, 137
light, 12, 13, 19, 37, 38, 135-137
pearl of great value, 102, 103
Penington, Isaac, 22, 49, 121
Quakerism, Catholic, see Benson, Lewis
Quakers, see Friends
reactions, anniversary, 73, 75, 76, 78, 79,

88, 91, 105, 106, 109, 115, 129, 131

Satan, 64, 71, 80, 92, 99, 121, 122, 136

Scriptures, Scriptural, 11, 12, 19, 21, 135, 136

self-control, 29, 46, 60, 63-66, 69-71, 77

sin(s), 4, 48, 57-61, 64, 65, 71, 128

Sodom and Gamorrah, 5

splits, denominational, 23

tempt, temptation, 80, 92, 105, 128

Testament, New, 1, 5, 10-12, 18, 52, 67, 92, 100-102, 121, 124, 125, 128

Testament, Old, 5, 40, 57

trials, 11, 79-81, 96, 103, 131

unity, 23, 25